Alexander Hamilton

A Captivating Guide to an American Founding Father Who Wrote the Majority of The Federalist Papers

Free Bonus from Captivating History (Available for a Limited time)

Hi History Lovers!

Now you have a chance to join our exclusive history list so you can get your first history ebook for free as well as discounts and a potential to get more history books for free! Simply visit the link below to join.

Captivatinghistory.com/ebook

Also, make sure to follow us on Facebook, Twitter and Youtube by searching for Captivating History.

Contents

Introduction

Alexander Hamilton, unlike many of the other Founding Fathers of the United States, was born outside of wedlock and was an orphan at the age of thirteen after his mother died. He and his brother grew up in the West Indies on the islands of Nevis and Saint Croix, which are now part of the Virgin Islands. They spoke French on Nevis, which is where he was born. Alexander's mother, Rachel, ran away from her legal husband, James Lavien, because he terrorized her. She later met John Hamilton and lived with him in a common-law relationship. They had two boys—Alexander and James. When his business went bad, John abandoned Rachel and the two boys who were just in their pre-teens. She ran a small shop supplying sailors for their trips abroad, and she managed with the money she had.

In February 1768, his mother died of yellow fever, after which her legal husband returned and confiscated everything they owned, which the law allowed at the time. There they were, two adolescents thrown into the world, depending on the charity of friends and neighbors. That perhaps is one of the reasons why Alexander Hamilton was fiscally sensitive and always anxious about funding and finance, not only for himself but for the new nation of the United States, where he emigrated when he was in his late teens. It is no wonder then that he became the first Secretary of the Treasury of the United States and that he even saved banks from financial collapse.

His home island of Nevis was a rough place to live. Gruff sailors covered with brine frequented the port that he lived by where frightened African slaves were sold in the market square. Life there was based on survival, and Alexander Hamilton's first occupation in his new country of the United States was as a military officer. He was brash and fearless. It was he that stood along with General George Washington during the surrender of General Charles Cornwallis at Yorktown, Virginia.

Hamilton had a brilliant mind. Although the law was his calling, he was blessed with charisma that could persuade even the stoniest of hearts. As a prolific writer, he never shied from presenting his legal (and personal) opinions regarding the political issues of the day.

Temperamentally, he was a warm and cordial companion but could effectively rebut anyone who disagreed with him, and—for some reason—he was always surprised when he lost. Hamilton, unfortunately or fortunately, was brutally honest and told everyone what he thought. People like that can attract many friends but just as many enemies. Politically, he was a Federalist in support of a strong national government but would occasionally support a rival candidate if he felt that the rival candidate would do a better job for the country. He gave up any presidential ambitions he had for himself due to a highly publicized illicit affair, but he continued as an expert campaigner and powerbroker for others. His resiliency was truly astounding.

Alexander Hamilton and Aaron Burr, a banker and an entrepreneur, were political rivals for nearly fifteen years. After running for president along with Jefferson and being relegated to becoming just vice president, Burr attempted to run as the governor of New York. Hamilton then vociferously opposed him. When Burr lost that election, he blamed Hamilton and challenged him to the most historical duel of the 19th century. As a result, Hamilton died, and a country mourned him. However, his legacy lives on.

Chapter 1 – From Nevis to Boston

Nevis was once a tropical island with luscious plants spotted with brightly colored flowers dripping nectar onto the rich soil, but that was gone after it was settled. Instead, it became a place of devastation. In the 1750s, Nevis was under the possession of the King of Norway and Denmark. The indigenous people were the dark-skinned Nevisians ruled over by Chief Tegremond until Denmark took possession of the island. The Europeans there were French Huguenots who had escaped France when they were being persecuted because of their religion. Dr. John Fawcett, Hamilton's grandfather, was a French Huguenot—a Protestant reformer who rejected the domination of Catholicism in 17th-century France. About him, Hamilton wrote, "My grandfather by my mother's side of the name of Fawcett was a French Huguenot who emigrated to the West Indies in consequence of the revocation of the Edict of Nantes and settled in the island of Nevis…he practiced as a physician." The family records are poor, as the name "Fawcett" is also spelled as "Faucett," "Fawcette," and even "Fosset" on some documents. On this tropical island, John Fawcett met Mary Uppington, an Anglican, and married her. Besides practicing medicine, John was a gentleman farmer and lived from circa 1680 to 1745.

After Dr. John Fawcett died, he left quite a bit of money to his sons and daughters, including Rachel, Hamilton's mother. In 1745,

Rachel and her mother Mary moved to the nearby island of Saint Croix (currently one of the U.S. Virgin Islands). While there, Rachel was approached by a man named Johann Michael Lavien. He was very dazzled by Rachel's lovely clothes and thought she was independently wealthy, so he fancied that he could buy a sugar plantation and become a respected landowner. Rachel already owned sixteen slaves from the indigenous population, which Lavien imagined he could use for his potential plantation. Anxious to have her daughter marry into wealth, her mother, Mary, persuaded Rachel to marry Lavien. She followed her mother's advice, and they had a son, Peter, in 1746, but the marriage was a rocky one. Lavien was an avaricious and cruel man. Unable to tolerate his abuse any longer, Rachel complained bitterly and ran away in 1750. After locating her, Rachel's vengeful husband imprisoned her at Fort Christiansted in Saint Croix, which was a practice under Danish law for a disobedient wife. After her stint in confinement, Rachel was still so frightened of her husband that she abandoned him and their young child and fled to the island of Nevis just west of there.

Rachel never returned home and escaped to the British West Indies—a chain of islands just northwest of there. There, she met James A. Hamilton, a Scottish merchant and entrepreneur. They fell in love with each other, and he took her to the island of St. Kitts and later back to Nevis.

However, there was a problem. Rachel was still legally married to Johann Michael Lavien, so the Scottish Presbyterians wouldn't recognize a marriage between Hamilton and Rachel Fawcett Lavien. Thus, they cohabited. In 1753, they gave birth to a son, James Jr., and on January 11th, 1755 (or 1757), they gave birth to Alexander. Once Rachel's husband, Johann Michael Lavien, heard about this in 1759, he divorced Rachel on the grounds of desertion. James Hamilton called Lavien a "fortune hunter, bedizened with gold." Rachel and her common-law husband did well together until James Hamilton experienced a severe downturn in his business and disappeared.

Years later, Alexander wrote to his brother, James Jr., asking, "But what has become of our dear father? It is an age since I have heard from him though I have written…I entreat you, if you can, to relieve my doubts, and let me know how or where he is, if alive, if dead, how and where he died." His brother didn't have any definitive information, but family records later revealed that Alexander's father wrote to him from the island of Bequia in the Grenadines in 1786. That group of islands lies southeast of Nevis, very close to the shore of South America. According to the records, the young men found out that their father sold his lot of land and moved 100 miles northward, settling on the island of St. Vincent. He never made any effort to contact his two boys again.

Rachel's Unfortunate Legacy

Rachel was now left to care for her two sons by herself. She rented out a shop in Christiansted from which she sold clothing, plantation equipment, and supplies for the sailors and planters. She and her two boys, when they were old enough, worked hard, and they were able to buy some furniture and silverware for their modest dwelling. Because of the religious laws, children from illegitimate marriages were forbidden from receiving an education in the Anglican church schools. Thus, Rachel enlisted private tutors and paid for that by teaching classes at a local Jewish school.

Although this island would normally appear to be a virtual paradise for vacationers, it wasn't. This was a relatively poor area full of people who were struggling for survival. Many of the Nevisians were slaves, and they worked the plantations for a handful of wealthy planters who separated themselves from the populace. Luckily, the slaves and the freed Nevisians were often given Sundays off and sold some of their handmade wares in the street markets. Freed slaves had larger stalls there and ran their businesses in the heart of the busy port city.

The cargo that traversed this port sometimes carried disease, particularly yellow fever. That disease was quite common in the 18th

century as it could be easily carried from African monkeys and mosquitoes. In the year 1768, both Alexander and his mother contracted it. The illness bypassed James Jr. for reasons unknown. Both Alexander and his mother underwent primitive 18th-century treatments—bloodletting, enemas, and the use of a risky herbal product, valerian, which adversely affects the liver. Alexander survived the yellow fever, but the primitive treatments his mother was subjected to were ineffective, and she died on February 19th before the sun had even risen. Now, Alexander and James Jr. were orphans. As soon as Rachel's estranged husband, Johann Michael Lavien, received word of her demise, the avaricious man went to probate court and claimed the rights to his wife's money and goods, showing no interest in the two boys. Because Rachel had deserted him, the court awarded everything to Lavien. The two dazed boys were at the mercy of their friends and what relatives they had. Their nearest relative was a cousin, Peter Lytton of Saint Croix, and he donated the black drape for Rachel's coffin. Lytton then had a parish clerk conduct a brief funeral. As she wasn't permitted burial in a church cemetery, he had her buried on his property on the outskirts of Christiansted. The court then made James Jr. and Alexander wards of Peter Lytton and his wife, Ann, Rachel's sister. Lytton, like so many of the planters in the region, ran into setbacks on his plantation and went into heavy debt. The court records reported that Lytton became totally despondent and either "stabbed or shot himself to death" in July of 1769. Lacking foresight, what goods and cash Peter still had was bequeathed to his mistress, Ledja, and their mulatto son. Unfortunately for Hamilton and his brother, Peter Lytton's brother, James, died shortly thereafter, so the boys were at the mercy of poor Ledja who couldn't support them. Because Peter was bankrupt at the time of his demise, he also left nothing in his will to his wife or the boys, either. History has no record of what happened to Ledja and her son, but James Jr. and Alexander Hamilton were now wards of the state.

Clerkship

After Peter's death, a local carpenter, Thomas McNobeny, took in James as an apprentice, and a Scottish merchant, Thomas Stevens, oversaw Alexander's upbringing. Only the landowners and larger import-export offices brought in a decent income that could help in the support of the boys. Everyone else on the island was either engaged in menial work in the fields or labored in the counting houses of clerks and money changers.

Auctions were held under the tents in the sandy streets of Christiansted. There were many import-export businesses in the busy port, including that of Beekman and Cruger, who later became Kortright and Cruger. Nicholas Cruger saw some promise in Alexander and created an apprenticeship for him. Alexander came across as precocious and intelligent and was excited about being able to work. Cruger then apprenticed Alexander to his establishment to work alongside his own son on Saint Croix. Kortright and Cruger was an import-export firm which conducted business between New England and New York, as well as to the French West Indies. Alexander was a little under thirteen years old at the time, and his role was that of a clerk. Unfortunately, he hated the work, although he performed it well. While there, Alexander admitted to his older foster brother, Edward Stevens, "I condemn the groveling condition of a clerk, or the like, to which my fortune condemns me, and would willingly risk my life though not my character, to exalt my station."

In time, however, Cruger noted that Hamilton was capable of much more than just bookkeeping, and he permitted him to do more work. Young men during the 18th century were often entrusted with a great deal of responsibility during their years as apprentices. Fortunately, Alexander was left in charge of his employer's office when Edward Stevens was away, which gave him broader experience. He was able to handle the bills of lading, the inspection of cargo, and even advised the ship's captains.

Alexander was very pleased with this added responsibility and often wandered about the port, which was packed with clipper ships and sloops carrying rum, sugar, grain, flour, and even timber. Besides the traditional trade that kept this port extremely active, the docks were also replete with smugglers. That secretive collection of swarthy-looking men not only smuggled in contraband but engaged in slave trading under the authority of the import-export company Hamilton worked for. Occasionally, notices appeared in the *Royal Danish Gazette*: "Just imported from the windward coast of Africa and to be sold on Monday next by Mssrs. Kortright & Cruger at said Cruger's yard, three hundred prime slaves." Alexander looked upon these unfortunate black men dragged up from the cargo hold of their ships and put on display to sell to the highest bidder. Most were naked, drenched in sweat, and terrified. Having been confined to close quarters below deck, they were blinded by the bright light of the tropical sun and bent over, squinting. Alexander immediately felt sympathy and treated them decently but realized he was helpless in terms of resolving their dilemma.

Hamilton and the other young men in the region were required to enlist in the local militia. There were a number of revolts and rebellions in the area, as the islands attracted a motley group of foreigners. In addition to that, there were slave rebellions, and Hamilton had to fight with the other members of the militia in order to quell them. He wasn't unsympathetic to their struggles, but he was given no choice when he was ordered to attack them during a revolt. After seeing the cruelties imposed upon these slaves, Hamilton thought of his own impoverished beginnings and was deathly afraid he, too, might meet their fate. Their lowly position in life instilled in him a fear of never being able to elevate himself above his own station and becoming as needy as the slaves. Hamilton had to survive on his wits and his desperate need to make a living in a harsh environment.

Hamilton's only escape was his fervent intellect and imagination. He read and consumed the printed word like a glutton. Books took him to other places where life might be more palatable. He even penned a few short poems, which were accepted for publication in the *Royal Danish Gazette*. For one of his submissions, he decided to write a piece about a hurricane that ravaged the island. Saint Croix was subject to a great many vicious hurricanes, but the hurricane of 1772 was particularly horrifying. Below follows a portion of that essay:

> Good God! What horror and destruction—it's impossible for me to describe—or you to form any idea of it. It seemed as if a total dissolution of nature was taking place. The roaring of the sea and wind—fiery meteors flying about in the air—the prodigious glare of almost perpetual lightning—the crash of the falling houses—and the ear-piercing shrieks of the distressed, were sufficient to strike astonishment into angels.

Then he showed it to the pastor of a Scottish Presbyterian church he occasionally attended, Reverend Hugh Knox. Knox was astounded by the sophistication of Hamilton's writing style and said that he would submit it to the *Royal Danish Gazette* for Alexander and enclosed a letter written by Hamilton that said:

> I am afraid, Sir, you will think this description more the effort of imagination than a true picture of realities. But I can affirm with the greatest truth, that there is not a single circumstance touched upon, which I have not absolutely been an eyewitness to.

Knox was well aware that the Church wasn't supposed to educate illegitimate children, but he considered that policy unfair and took a special interest in Alexander. So, he tutored him in the sciences and humanities. Knox had a large library, and Alexander took full advantage of it. When he wasn't working, Hamilton read some of the works of Alexander Pope, a poet of that day, and Plutarch, the Greek-Roman chronicler. Reverend Knox then started a fund to send Alexander to the United States. Many people in the community, including Hamilton's firm of Kortright and Cruger, financed him to go to the colonies in British America for a proper education. They knew this boy was special and that his talents should be employed toward more productive ends.

Boston

The "West Indian boy," as he was known, arrived in the port of Boston in October of 1772 and was met by Hugh Mulligan, a customer of the Cruger firm where Hamilton had worked. Through Hugh, Hamilton met Hugh's brother, Hercules Mulligan, when he moved to New York and Hercules offered him lodging there. Hercules then arranged for Alexander to take some college preparatory courses at Elizabethtown Academy in New Jersey in 1773. There, Hamilton met the illustrious William Livingston, who shared the same religious faith with him, that of Presbyterianism. Livingston was a wealthy man and was in the process of building an estate there, now called Liberty Hall. Hamilton was then boarding at Elizabethtown Academy and often visited Livingston, as did many of the other young men from the academy. In the winter, Hamilton even lived with the Livingstons. Following his term at Elizabethtown, Hamilton applied to the College of New Jersey (later Princeton University) on the condition that he would be put on the fast-track as he wanted to complete his education as soon as possible. They turned him down because of that condition, but he had simultaneously applied to King's College (currently Columbia University) in New York and was accepted in 1773 as a special student.

During the early 1770s, there were rumors and whispers about rebellion against the British control of the colonies. There were political unrest and protests due to the increase of taxes levied upon them. In the taverns and on the college campuses, colonists began to split into camps—those who supported British domination were known as the Loyalists and those who fostered rebellion were known as the Patriots. Hamilton had come from a background of repression in Nevis and Saint Croix, and here was a country that promised more freedom and opportunity. Alexander—while attending the King's College—formed a debating club. He was incensed by the offenses against the rights of the colonists and was tired of being simply a victim of his circumstances.

In late 1772, the British East India Company, which imported tea to America, was in financial straits. Tea was the most popular beverage in America, and the British levied a tea tax upon the colonists to make up for the shortfall. The colonists had already been incensed at the fact that they had no representation in the British Parliament, and they now realized that they had no control at all over the export taxes they remitted to Great Britain. When the Patriots dumped barrels of tea overboard into the Boston Harbor in December 1773 at the event later called the "Boston Tea Party," Hamilton cheered and presented an energetic appeal to his debating club members, saying that such protests "will prove the salvation of North America and her liberties," otherwise "fraud, power, and the most odious oppression will rise triumphant over social happiness and freedom." When Hamilton heard the contrary opinions of the president of King's College, Myles Cooper, he was astonished because he had always respected Cooper's viewpoints. Cooper wished for the country to continue to be subservient to Great Britain. At one time, Cooper was even heard to have called the people of Boston a "crooked and perverse generation," adding that their colonial charter should be rescinded. That puzzled Hamilton, who had always considered himself to be a good judge of character.

Following the Boston Tea Party, the colonies elected delegates to meet in Philadelphia and discuss how to deal with Britain's oppressive actions. This assembly became known as the Continental Congress, and William Livingston himself was elected as a representative.

Hamilton's college president, Myles Cooper, was among a group of Loyalists who were very active in their opposition to that congress. One member of Cooper's inner circle was another Anglican minister, Samuel Seabury, who published a retort about the impropriety of holding such meetings in a long pamphlet called *Free Thoughts on the Proceedings of the Continental Congress held at Philadelphia,*

Sept. 5, 1774; Wherein their errors are exhibited, their reasonings confuted. Seabury signed the lengthy thesis "A. W. Farmer," and it was published in the *New York Gazetteer*. In this, Seabury states:

> Will you choose such committees? Will you submit to them should they be chosen by the weak, foolish, turbulent part of the country people? Do as you please, but by HIM that made me, I will not. No, if I must be enslaved, let it be by a KING at least and not by a parcel of upstart lawless Committeemen.

In 1775, while he was still attending college, Hamilton, who was never averse to controversy, anonymously wrote *A Full Vindication of the Measures of the Congress from the calumnies of their enemies in answer to A Letter under the signature of A. W. Farmer*. In it, he moved to a discussion of the rights of man to make his own choices, questioning very directly:

> What then is the subject of our controversy with the mother country—It is this: whether we shall preserve that security to our lives and properties which the law of nature and the genius of the British constitution and our colonial charters afford us, or whether we shall resign them into the hands of the British House of Commons, which is no more privileged to dispose of them than the Grand Mogul?

Chapter 2 – From Pen to Sword

It took only four days for Hamilton and his classmates in New York to hear the news that the port of Boston was closed to all but British warships. Then Hamilton and his colleagues from college got word about a clash between the British regiments and the patriotic militia from Boston, the Minutemen. General Thomas Gage, the British Governor of Massachusetts Bay Colony, had infiltrated the interior of the colony in search of hidden caches of weapons. The Minutemen, aided by patriotic locals, followed the British regiments through Concord, and a deadly conflict broke out in Lexington on April 19th, 1775. What Hamilton and his classmates heard was that the losses of the British numbered 73 and 49 Patriots lay dead near a bridge crossing.

Anger erupted amongst the colonists, and on April 24th, thousands of students and New Yorkers protested at city hall. In May, a group who knew that Hamilton's college president, Myles Cooper, had Loyalist leanings rushed into his campus residence. An alumnus by the name of Nicholas Ogden woke Cooper, and the frightened man in his nightcap peered out the window. Even though he had political differences with Myles Cooper, Hamilton and his friend, Robert

Troup, didn't feel that he deserved to be injured. So, he and Troup held off the mob on the stairway. Hamilton hollered to the crowd that violence against this defenseless man would only hurt their cause. His words weren't entirely effective, but it allowed Cooper enough time to escape and rush toward the Hudson River. After wandering around all night in his nightclothes, Cooper came upon a British warship, boarded it, and headed back to England!

Many colonists still discussed the possibility of reconciliation with Great Britain. Hamilton picked up his pen again and sent out some bold letters against reconciliation that were published in the *New York Gazetteer*. That newspaper was a Loyalist-leaning paper, but it often printed letters from the Patriots, as it had done in the "A. W. Farmer" letters. The Rivington Press, which published the *Gazetteer*, was destroyed by an angry mob, and the presses were damaged beyond repair. Afterward, a sign was placed outside the shop which read, "The printing of the *New York Gazetteer* will be discontinued until America shall be blessed with the restoration of good government." Hamilton had been upset by the pending attack on Myles Cooper, and now he felt the same about the livelihood of James Rivington, the printer. He wrote to John Jay, a well-known statesman who had married William Livingston's daughter. Jay was from New York and was also a delegate to the First Continental Congress. Hamilton said to Jay that although he felt the newspaper was detestable, he was concerned about the lawless nature of the colonists' retaliation.

Hamilton spoke to some of the other students at King's College, and they decided to join a newly forming militia. The militia drilled behind St. Paul's Chapel, which was nearby. The militia called itself the "Corsicans," later renamed the "Hearts of Oak." Every morning, Hamilton drilled with the other college volunteers under Edward Fleming, who used to be a captain in a British regiment.

Some of the Governors' Councils in the colonies had also been suspended by the British, so there was a need for a colonial-based assembly to recall the Continental Congress into its second session in May 1775. They called again upon delegates from each of the colonies to meet in Philadelphia to plan a course of action. The members of the assembly had no authority to govern but took it upon themselves to form a provisional government. They then circulated a resolution among the colonies advising that each should declare independence from Great Britain. After some discussion among the colonies, it was agreed to. Richard Lee of Virginia then proposed that the colonies as a unit declare themselves independent from Great Britain. So, the Articles of Confederation were drawn up, the group recognized the need to form foreign alliances for military aid, and a paper currency was issued called the Continental Dollar. Plans were then made to create a formal declaration of independence, and Thomas Jefferson, the prolific young writer from Virginia, was chosen to write it. At that meeting, George Washington, who had military experience while working under British commanders, was chosen as the Commander-in-Chief of the Continental Army. Word went out, and colonial recruits came from all parts of the colonies. Some even trained themselves, forming smaller units and looked for opportunities to join up with the main forces.

New York had established a local Provincial Congress and formed an artillery company to defend the colony. There, Hamilton met a friend of his, William Livingston. Hamilton not only had the experience from his college militia drills, but he had studied up on military tactics and told Livingston about it. Then he was introduced to Colonel Alexander McDougall, a Scotsman, who was pleased to hear about Hamilton's knowledge and even recommended that Hamilton be the captain of an artillery company. His college roommate, Robert Troup, also spoke with John Jay on Hamilton's behalf. Alexander Hamilton was then appointed the Captain of Artillery for the Provincial Government of New York. Hamilton then dropped out of school, but the school was suspended shortly thereafter at any rate because of the unrest in the colonies.

As a captain, Hamilton became popular with the men when he negotiated their pay, which was to be the same as the forces recruited for the regular Continental Army George Washington was forming.

On June 28th, 1776, George Washington discovered a traitor among his Continental Army, a man named Thomas Hickey. Hickey had organized a plot to murder Continental officers and revealed the location of colonists' magazines to the British, after which they were blown up. To make an example of him, Washington had him convicted of treason, and he was hanged at the Bowery in the southern area of Manhattan Island. Today, little is known of that event.

In July, Admiral Samuel Graves had now assumed command of a large number of British man-of-war ships, and they were sitting just below Manhattan at Sandy Hook, New Jersey, ready to stage an amphibious attack on Manhattan Island. In the meantime, Washington had gathered as many as 20,000 Continental troops. The newly formed army lacked sufficient ammunition, so Washington issued orders to remove any leaden window frames in order to melt them down to make bullets. To the northeast, the British commander, General William Howe, had his brother, Admiral Richard Howe, sail up through the Narrows in their warships. The Narrows is a deep waterway between Staten Island and Long Island paralleling the East River alongside Manhattan. Colonel McDougall made contact with General Washington and was told to station Captain Hamilton and his troops at the Battery, located at the southern tip of Manhattan. From their vantage point, they could observe the whole action.

On July 12th, Captain Hamilton was confronted with a 44-gun battleship, the *Phoenix*, and a 28-gun frigate, the *Rose*, with its guns firing. Hamilton's artillery unit fired incessantly upon the ships, and then Hamilton had his men light the cannons. To the horror of his soldiers, the cannons malfunctioned, blowing up six of his own men and wounding others. Due to the lack of experience of many of his men, more mishaps occurred. Hamilton was emotionally crushed by this circumstance and rapidly learned that war was a dirty and brutal business and hardly a reliable one.

Washington's ragtag troops were scattered in fortifications built up on Brooklyn Heights at the southern end of Long Island. However, thousands of British and the mercenary Hessian troops penetrated those defenses, threatening the lives of the people living there. The British had at least twice as many enemy forces than the Continental Army had at that time.

In August, Hamilton, under the Continental Artillery Captain John Lamb, ordered the seizure of 24 cannons from the Battery. They stole up the shore and started dragging the cannons away, but a Loyalist had given the British advance warning. The British then opened fire on Hamilton and his men from a barge they had just offshore. Hamilton and his unit returned fire but kept tugging on the cannons. Hercules Mulligan, whom Hamilton had roomed with in New York, was also in his regiment, and the two fought side by side during this action. As a result of their efforts, Hamilton and Mulligan were able to take 21 of the 24 cannons, which they dragged uptown to city hall.

Stealthily, Washington and his troops in Brooklyn Heights were forced to make a nighttime retreat. The British then pillaged their farms and devastated the countryside of Brooklyn, which Washington had to abandon because there was nothing he could do to stop them.

Washington and his troops then marched to White Plains, New York. The Americans dug in around the base of Chatterton Hill and planted themselves in various positions up the hill. Hamilton mounted the hill and placed his 2-gun battery at the top. The British then moved in from Brooklyn Heights, swarming the area, and began climbing the hill. Every time the British made any progress, they were beaten back by the Americans toward the nearby town of Sleepy Hollow. In the course of their halting progress, the head of one of the Hessians was blown off, and that gave rise to "The Legend of Sleepy Hollow," which is about a headless horseman who haunts the region.

Later in the battle, Colonel Johann Rall joined up with the British forces with thousands of more men. Ferociously, they split up Hamilton's militia, who were forced to cross the Bronx River and rejoin Washington's main division in the hills.

Following that, Lieutenant-General Hugh Percy also arrived, thus reinforcing the British, and they planned on surrounding Washington. However, a driving rain fell, and they were forced to delay their plans. That was fortunate for Washington and his men, who would have been hopelessly outnumbered and defeated but were now offered the opportunity to retreat.

Surreptitiously, Hamilton and his men kept calm during the orderly retreat, crossing the Hudson River and moving into New Jersey. As they moved southward, Washington reorganized his men and posted young Hamilton high on the riverbanks with rifles drawn to pick off the British who were likely to pursue them downstate. Hamilton directed volleys against columns of British regiments marching on the lower ground. They were headed toward the Raritan River on the way to the capital city of Trenton, New Jersey.

Washington had Hamilton hold up the rear of his forces, and they moved west across New Jersey, marching southward from New Brunswick and crossing the Delaware River and encamping alongside it. They were then directly west of the Hessians, who were stationed at a garrison nearby. The enemy was celebrating at the home of a Loyalist in Trenton the day after Christmas. Captain Hamilton and his associate, Captain Forrest, took their artillery company and covered King's Street and Queen's Street which led into the city. Then Washington and his men began their attack. Hamilton and Forrest—along with Edward Hand's Pennsylvanian units—fired upon the garrison, and Lieutenant Andreas Weiderhold hollered out "Der Feind!" ("The Enemy!"), summoning his soldiers who came rushing out. Hamilton and the other Continental troops met heavy action on lower King's Street and Queen's Street. They killed and captured hundreds of them. During the street fighting, the commander of the second unit of the Hessian divisions, Johann Rall, was fatally wounded. This battle, known as the Battle of Trenton, was a tremendous victory for the Patriots. The Continental forces then moved back to the Pennsylvania side of the river to plan their next strategy. Washington and his officers felt that an attack on Lieutenant-General Charles Cornwallis and Lieutenant-Colonel Charles Mawhood at Princeton would be feasible.

In January of 1777, Washington's troops awoke in the middle of the night then secretly sailed back across the Delaware River. From there, his forces moved northeast along the trail called the Post Road toward Princeton and spotted the British. Washington shouted to his men, "It's a fox chase, my boys!" Hamilton's 5th regiment, along with the Virginia Continentals, pounded the British under Lieutenant-Colonel Mawhood. The British fell in such large numbers that Mawhood ordered a retreat. Most of the British soldiers followed Mawhood outside of Princeton, but a smaller unit rushed down the street and hid in Nassau Hall, the city administration building. Hamilton grabbed his cannons, collected his men outside the structure, and pommeled the building. Some of Hamilton's men then stormed the door and broke it down. A white flag waved from one of the windows, and 194 of the British soldiers surrendered. It was yet another triumph for the Continental Army. After the battle, a senior officer remarked about Hamilton, "I noticed a youth, a mere stripling, small, slender with a cocked hat pulled down over his eyes, apparently lost in thought, with his hand resting on a cannon, and every now and then patting it, as if it was a favorite horse or pet plaything."

Washington encamped at various places in New Jersey, moving about frequently to avoid detection. In the spring of 1777, Washington was moving southward along the eastern border of Pennsylvania. Hamilton and his artillery force were then ordered to take possession of a flour warehouse so the British couldn't seize it.

As he was riding, Hamilton's horse was shot out from under him, and he had to swim across the Schuylkill River to rejoin Washington.

Washington later sent young Hamilton to secure reinforcements to protect some of the areas around Philadelphia. Hamilton approached General Horatio Gates with the request. After Gates selected a brigade, Hamilton noted that the very small body of men Gates gave him had all the earmarks of being new recruits, so he demanded more troops with experience as well. Gates was astonished at Hamilton's brashness, but he also realized that this young man wasn't easily fooled and responded with what Hamilton knew was needed.

Hamilton as an Aide de Camp

Washington was impressed with Hamilton's performance in Brooklyn, Trenton, and Princeton. Desirous of having this brave and brash young man continue to serve with him, Washington promoted Hamilton to the rank of lieutenant-colonel. John Laurens from South Carolina as well as Aaron Burr from New Jersey were also aides-de-camp. All of them were not only skilled militarily but had clerical knowledge and could write well. Hamilton and the others served under Washington for four years and worked with intelligence operations, negotiations, diplomacy, and served as his emissaries as well. Hamilton served as Washington's aide-de-camp from 1777 to 1781.

In the year 1777, the French military colonel Marquis de Lafayette arrived with forces to help in the effort, even though France wasn't officially an ally yet. Washington knew that Hamilton spoke French fluently because his mother was a French Huguenot, so he had the Marquis speak with Hamilton on his behalf. In time, Hamilton befriended Lafayette, and the French Marquis even spent time with Hamilton and his family several years later.

During the Revolutionary War, they marched alongside each other throughout New Jersey. At the Battle of Monmouth on June 28th,

1778, they parted company temporarily when Burr and Laurens had their horses shot out from under them. Laurens recovered, but Burr had been more severely injured, so it took him more time.

The Battle of Monmouth took place near the Monmouth Courthouse in New Jersey. When the Continental Army was near the courthouse, Washington's officers suggested various actions they might engage in against the British troops, under Sir Henry Clinton, who were in the area. General Charles Lee felt that it might be better to subject the British to running skirmishes, which would use far fewer men. Washington then sent out Hamilton to assess the situation. Hamilton reported back that the British army was quite formidable there and would require a huge number of Continental forces along with supportive forces to back them up in order to achieve victory, saying to Washington, "To attack in this situation without being supported by the whole army at a distance, would be folly in the extreme." Instead, Hamilton suggested an attack on the British rearguard. Lee, on the other hand, was convinced that the British were practically invincible, and it would be far better just to harass them and kill the stragglers. Washington thought about it and then ordered Lee to attack with 5,000 men with a backup force under the Marquis de Lafayette, who was about a mile away. During the course of the Battle of Monmouth, Hamilton noted that the British were reinforcing their flank, so he sent word to the Marquis de Lafayette to join up with him. Rather than stay in the fight while waiting for Lafayette's reinforcements, though, Lee and his group retreated. Washington was furious and took off looking for Lee. Finding him, Washington insisted Lee make a stand. After the Battle of Monmouth, the British proclaimed a victory, but so did the Americans. The results of this battle were inconclusive, leading to no clear advantage on either side.

Hamilton was so dissatisfied by the conduct of Lee that he felt that Lee was either "a driveler in the business of soldiership or something worse." When Lee heard that, he wrote a letter to Washington and demanded a court-martial against Hamilton. Henry Laurens, his fellow officer and friend, testified along with Hamilton that Lee participated in a disgraceful retreat that was neither necessary nor ordered. As a result of the court-martial, Lee was reprimanded and convicted on three counts: 1) disobedience to orders, 2) misbehavior in making an unnecessary, disorderly, and shameful retreat, and 3) disrespect to the commander-in-chief. He was found guilty on all three counts, and he was suspended from the army for a year.

After the war, Lee went to Philadelphia and published his "Vindication," "damning George Washington…and congress." He also struck hard against Hamilton and Laurens, calling them Washington's "hatchet men."

Hamilton and Laurens became very close friends. In a letter to Laurens in 1779, Hamilton said to him, "I have written you five times since I left Philadelphia and I should have written you more had you made proper return. But like a jealous lover when I thought you slighted my caresses, my affection was alarmed and vanity piqued." Some speculate the two might have been involved in a homosexual relationship, although there isn't enough evidence for this to be proven.

In the position as Washington's aide-de-camp, Hamilton was in the midst of all the jealousies and politicking of the men who frequented Washington's offices. During that time, Hamilton also kept a close watch on the naïve Continental Congress and was critical of those who were individualistic and favored states' rights over that of a strong national government. Hamilton always expressed himself freely and made his opinions known among his contemporaries. Sometimes that got him into trouble, especially when people exaggerated his words or put a negative spin on what he said. In a coffee shop in Philadelphia, someone spread the rumor that Hamilton said, "It was high time for the people to rise, join George Washington, and turn congress out of doors." Of course, he had said no such thing, but there were many who were envious of Washington's fondness for Hamilton. Many politicians considered

Hamilton to be no more than an ignorant military officer who "needed to be put in his place."

When these stories circulated, Hamilton suspected that the sources were from the supporters and friends of General Charles Lee, who was humiliated after the court-martial. Meticulously, Hamilton traced the story to Francis Dana, a member of the Continental Congress. Dana, however, claimed he heard it from Reverend William Gordon, who regularly sent Washington advice about the war. He loved scandals and gossip, and he frequently spread falsities. Once he even accused another aide-de-camp, Joseph Reed, of promoting the support of Charles Lee as a replacement for George Washington as the commander-in-chief.

Gordon repeated the rumor that Hamilton had denigrated Congress at the Philadelphia coffee shop, and then in 1778, he boldly wrote to Washington that "You have some treacherous person about you that betrays you and our officers to the enemy." Hamilton knew Gordon was referring to him.

Gordon had secretly hoped that perhaps Washington would hire him to be a spy to ferret out subversives in the troops. Washington was impatient and annoyed with this, calling it "tittle-tattle" that would only delay their business of war. However, the politicians in those days were incurable gossip-mongers, and Washington's words did little to stop the spread of rumors.

Marriage

While Hamilton functioned as Washington's aide-de-camp, he was stationed near Morristown, New Jersey, during their winter encampment there in 1780. Eliza Schuyler, a New York socialite, had been staying with her aunt nearby during this time. Hamilton had met her briefly at the Schuyler Mansion in Albany when he had been meeting with some dignitaries on Washington's behalf. Hamilton wanted to marry into wealth. In fact, he even asked for a marital reference from his friend, John Laurens. He said to John, "She must be young, handsome (I lay most stress upon a good shape) sensible (a little learning will do), well-bred. On politics, I am indifferent as to what side she shall be on, I have arguments that will easily convert her to mine." Those charismatic qualities of his served Hamilton well throughout his life and did much to determine his motivations and political drive.

Eliza was wealthy, as her father, Philip, was a rich slave trader. Hamilton had nothing by the way of money or land but pursued her nevertheless. Hamilton had met her several times at the Schuyler mansion. Although Hamilton's efforts were fruitless, he kept up a correspondence with Eliza. Hamilton was bright and charming, and Eliza's father was impressed with him, despite the fact that Hamilton wasn't from a wealthy family. Therefore, he didn't mind the disparity in their social statuses.

While Hamilton was stationed with Washington at Morristown, New Jersey, Eliza was staying with her aunt nearby, and Hamilton enjoyed her company whenever he had the opportunity. Eliza became intrigued with Alexander, and by April, she and Hamilton were engaged.

Hamilton, as an aide-de-camp, resumed his duties at Morristown. Then it came to pass that Major John André was captured in a plot with Benedict Arnold to capture West Point and was charged with treason. Eliza told Hamilton that she had a crush on him as a young girl, and she asked Hamilton to intercede on his behalf. In order to impress Elizabeth, Hamilton interceded and asked for mercy for André after he was captured.

They took a very brief honeymoon, after which Eliza joined Hamilton in New Windsor, near Trenton. During their downtime, Eliza and Hamilton worked together on some of his political writings, including financial advice for Robert Morris, a Patriot and merchant who oversaw some of the procurement of supplies for the war.

Alexander and Eliza had eight children. Their first son, Philip, was born in 1782, and in 1783, they moved to Wall Street, which was in a wealthy area of New York City. Hamilton had his eye on status. A year later, they gave birth to a daughter, Angelica, a sensitive child who stayed with the Schuylers in Albany during the war. They had six other children after that, including John Church Hamilton, who wrote his father's biography.

Hamilton at the Siege of Yorktown

As his work became more clerical, Hamilton yearned to be given a field command. He then asked Washington if he could step down from his role as aide-de-camp and serve actively in February 1781. Although the president hesitated at first, he finally relented in March and assigned Hamilton to a light infantry unit under Lafayette which was bearing down on Yorktown, Virginia, in September of 1781. The British commander, Lieutenant-General Charles Cornwallis, was there, but the harbor was blocked in by the French fleets of Admiral de Grasse to protect the Continental forces inland. Cornwallis was low on supplies because he couldn't gain access to the shore and was desperate for help. He had been promised reinforcements from General Henry Clinton from up north, but they hadn't arrived yet.

Hamilton was in charge of deconstructing Redoubt No. 10, built by the British outside Yorktown. In order to do that, Hamilton's artillery needed to get within firing range of the British regulars. Feverishly, he had his Continental and French soldiers quietly sneak up the earthen domes of the redoubt and then rip apart the hastily constructed wooden fences and tear out the spikes meant to slow their advance. Upon reaching the top of the dome, Hamilton and his men stormed down on the British troops, shooting round after round from their muskets. Many of the surrounding redoubts were being simultaneously attacked. This action caught the trenched-in British by surprise, but the fight continued on for three more grueling days. On October 17th, a huge white flag was waved from Cornwallis' division, and it was over. A little over 155 British soldiers lay dead on the uneven field saturated with blood, littered with twisted metal and torn-up uniforms. 28 Americans and 60 French were killed. The

British band played "The World Turned Upside Down" as the two opposing sides met to declare the end of the hostilities on October 19th:

> A ragged band they called the Diggers
>
> Came to show the people's will
>
> They defied the landlords; they defied the law;
>
> There were the dispossessed
>
> Reclaiming what was theirs.

Alexander Hamilton and John Laurens were two of the junior officers who stood behind Washington at the official surrender ending the American Revolution.

Chapter 3 – Onset of Hamilton's Political Career

Now that the Revolutionary War was over, Hamilton resigned his military commission and studied law. He passed the bar in 1782—an amazing accomplishment in such a brief period of time. Hamilton was brilliant and took to the study of law rapidly. He voraciously studied one of the standard reference books in the field at the time, Sir William Blackstone's *Commentaries on the English Common Law*. He immediately attracted wealthy clients in his home state of New York, like maritime insurance companies and wealthy merchants. In 1779, New York passed "An Act for the Forfeiture and Sale of the Estates of Persons who have adhered to the Enemies of this State, and for declaring the Sovereignty of the People within the same," or, for short, the "Confiscation Law." By that law, whoever was convicted of loyalty to the British Crown forfeited their real and personal property, and the state was then permitted to seize and sell it. After the war, Hamilton realized that the country needed the former Loyalists, so he disagreed with this law and felt that they shouldn't be abandoned or exiled. Hamilton looked upon the former Loyalists as fodder for building a new nation whose central government had strength and was in support of the Federalist agenda, those who favored a strong central government. He looked upon these people as being able to help ensure the country didn't become just a weak confederation of states—each with their own agendas—which would most likely detract from the union. If an ex-Loyalist experienced success in this new nation, where his property rights were respected, he might indeed help them mature into a fully united America.

Another act passed in New York around this time was the Trespass Act of 1783. It allowed Patriots whose property had been seized or damaged by Loyalists or the British to collect damages. Hamilton defended clients accused of breaking those laws, regardless of whether they were Patriots or former Loyalists.

Of the cases Hamilton defended, three of them were landmark cases—*Lloyd v. Lewis* (1784), *Rutgers v. Waddington* (1784), and *Post v. Leonard* (1786). In the *Lloyd v. Lewis* case, Scudder Lewis was required to work John Lloyd's land for the British who had confiscated it during the war. Hamilton helped clarify the fact that a man—regardless of whether he was a Patriot or Loyalist—should not be convicted of aiding the enemy by virtue of the confiscation law because the land didn't belong to him and he worked it under duress. In the *Rutgers v. Waddington* case, the owner of a tavern, Eleanor Rutgers, was forced to flee her tavern when it was confiscated by the British. The tavern was then run by Mr. Joshua Waddington, who rented it from the British occupiers. In 1784, Rutgers sued Waddington for the rent. Hamilton defended Waddington and won the case by proving that the Treaty of Paris, signed on September 3rd, 1783, stipulated that the British were due the payments as a war debt. Furthermore, it trumped the Trespass Act in that case because it was a state law and in contradiction with the Treaty of Paris.

In the case between Anthony Post and James Leonard, Hamilton utilized the tool of judicial review, which calls for a reanalysis of the case by certified judges. In that case, Leonard had acquired the property after a judgment of forfeiture and proved it couldn't be confiscated after the fact.

Hamilton wrote two essays in *The Federalist Papers* regarding the confiscation law. In them, he said that in the case of a conflict, "the Constitution ought to be preferred to the statute."

The procedure of judicial review was later employed in the famous *Madison v. Marbury* case heard before the Supreme Court. When there is a constitutional collision between two mandates—one passed by a state and another by the U.S. Constitution—it is the constitutional law which prevails. Although there may be many cases meeting that criteria, even today, each of those cases needs to reach the level of the higher courts, perhaps even the Supreme Court, before a precedent can be established.

Aaron Burr and the Confiscation Acts

Aaron Burr disagreed with Hamilton's opinion. He felt that the properties that had been confiscated from the Loyalists during the Revolution should be redistributed among the Patriots and sold at a cut-rate price if the grantee wished. Along with other people, Burr seized property belonging to Loyalists. He was the grantee of 2 pieces of property at Trinity Church in southern Manhattan, 300 lots on Houston Street, and 3 shares of the Bank of New York. According to the new stipulation on the Confiscation Acts, Burr had to see to it that those lots were returned to the previous owners.

Congress of the Confederation

While Hamilton was practicing in New York, he was appointed as the New York representative for the newly forming Congress of the Confederation, or the Confederation Congress, to create federal laws for the new nation.

Briefly, there were thirteen articles:

1. The union shall be called the "United States of America."

2. Each state had its own powers in addition to those listed in the articles.

3. The union is a "league of friendship."

4. People may travel freely among the states, and criminals must be returned to their own states to face trials.

5. Each state had between two to seven members, and there is one vote per state.

6. The central government handles foreign relations, trade agreements, and declarations of war.

7. States may assign military ranks below that of general.

8. Money is to be raised by each state to support the central government.

9. Congress passes laws and handles foreign affairs like peace, war, and treaties.

10. A committee called the Committee of States acts for the central government when it's not in session.

11. Canada may join the union, if desired.

12. The union will pay war debts.

13. The Articles of Confederation will be perpetual unless altered by the states and Congress.

The Articles of Confederation were ratified on March 1st, 1781.

There were serious flaws with these articles. First of all, they emphasized the separation of the states, putting little weight upon the united aspect of the states and denying the central government the power it needed to enact measures passed by Congress. Although money came up in terms of paying war debts and supporting the central government, no method of collection nor enforcement was specified. It almost sounded as if such monies were to be donations. Hamilton, in 1780, indicted that the failure of the central government to regulate commerce resulted in a different procedure for buying and selling manufactured goods in each state. There was no court system established, save the fact that a criminal had to be returned to his or her own state. And each state had only one vote regardless of the size or population of the state.

Hamilton was unhappy with the weaknesses he saw in the articles, as he felt they didn't have sufficient power to run an entire nation. Early into the process, Hamilton disagreed with the proposed ideas, saying that "the confederation itself is defective and requires to be altered; it is neither fit for war, nor peace." While he understood that the states were oversensitive to having virtually no power of their own, he was also critical of the fact that a federal government that could do nothing but ask or recommend that the states provide sufficient resources to support an army and navy, pay for staff of learned men to analyze proposed legislation, or have any powers of enforcement would get nowhere. In 1780, he wrote a number of letters to James Duane, whom he knew through the Livingston family. Duane was a prominent lawyer, a member of Congress, and later became a senator in New York. Hamilton wrote to him saying,

> 1. The fundamental defect is a want of power in Congress…It may however be said that it has originated from three causes – an excess of the spirit of liberty which has made particular states show a jealousy of all power not in their own hands;
>
> 2. A diffidence in Congress of their own powers, by which they have been timid and indecisive in their resolutions, constantly making concessions to the states; and
>
> 3. A want of sufficient means at their disposal to answer public exigencies and fulfill their engagements with the army.

One of the cited flaws manifested itself almost immediately. Article 12 indicated that the union shall pay its war debt, but that didn't happen as planned.

The Newburgh Conspiracy

In March 1783, the army was encamped at Newburgh, New York. Many of the soldiers had yet to be paid and didn't receive the pension they'd been promised. Robert Morris, a wealthy financier who had been funding many of the military efforts, was now forced to take out loans, but he could no longer do so and still stay solvent. A delegation of influential officers, including Hamilton's friend General Alexander McDougall, and Robert Morris met with Congress regarding the matter.

Congress was divided on the issue, even though the treasury was empty. It was suggested that an "impost tax" be charged, but not all the states were willing to participate. General McDougall then sent out a letter under the pseudonym "Brutus," warning of a possible mutiny forming.

Washington got word of this crisis, and Hamilton advised him to intervene by manifesting his support of the military but to do it in a gentle way so that Congress would be coaxed to respond. Washington understood the impact of personally appearing before a crowd, so he rushed up to Newburgh to address the war veterans. The men were shocked by his unexpected visit. Washington addressed them courteously and asked them not to "sully the glory" they had attained and expressed full confidence in Congress. He then fumbled for his spectacles to read a letter and apologized to the men, saying, "Gentlemen, you must pardon me. I have grown old in the service of my country and now find that I am growing blind." This subtle chide won the day, and the crowd disbursed in shame. Everyone knew Washington never asked to be paid for his service.

Despite this protest, Congress failed to pass a tax twice—in 1783 and in 1785—to pay for this war debt.

Shays' Rebellion

In 1786, Massachusetts tried to resolve the issue of local war debt by levying a tax in the state. That tax was quite high—even higher than the taxes paid to Great Britain before the war. The farmers, mostly in western Massachusetts, had received some money from the state to compensate for expenses incurred during the war. However, it was insufficient. These farmers had taken out loans from the banks to plant new crops and hadn't yet found a profit on their harvest, so they couldn't make all their payments. Their Continental Dollars were now worthless because its value had diminished since the end of the war. They didn't have silver or gold to use as a form of currency either. Then the authorities in Boston started to arrest the deadbeats and begin foreclosure procedures. At first, the farmers attempted to resolve these issues in court, but the judges were denied entry by the angry mobs. An ex-soldier by the name of Daniel Shays rose up among them and took 600 armed men to shut down the main courthouse in Springfield. General William Shepard, head of the state militia, arrived and negotiated with Shays. Events quieted for a while after the Massachusetts legislature offered leniency in terms of loan repayments. They passed another bill setting stiff penalties for the rebels in custody and freed the sheriffs from responsibility if any insurgents were killed. That infuriated the public, and Governor James Bowdoin hired 4,400 troops under General Benjamin Lincoln.

The year was now 1787, and the rebellion had only escalated. The mob attempted to raid the Springfield arsenal but was met by General Shepard. Shepard's men fired above their heads at first but then shot some of the rebels. A section of the militia also assaulted a farmer along with his family in Groton.

Yet another rebel, Luke Day, and his men arrived to help out, and they were joined by Eli Parsons and 600 more men from the mountains. General Benjamin Lincoln then chased them northward, and the group finally disbursed by the end of August.

When John Hancock was elected governor, he pardoned the rebels. Hamilton and even Madison agreed that the national government needed to be stronger but that it also needed to establish fairer taxes; to them, the rebellion was the logical outcome of fiscal mismanagement. Although he rarely attended the sessions of Congress, Hancock attended the sessions related to the writing of the state constitution. This constitution was written by John Adams, and Hancock wholeheartedly approved of it. It was passed in 1780.

Trade Debt Crisis: Tariff Wars

Those states that had ports found it necessary to impose duties and tariffs on vessels that docked there for the purpose of conducting trade. That included not only foreign ships but those from other states. Bias entered into the system when some ports set up protectionist trade barriers between certain states which they perceived as being in direct competition with products manufactured from their own respective states. For example, the port of New York imposed clearance fees for ships also trading with New Jersey.

In 1786, at the behest of James Madison, a young statesman from Virginia, a meeting of representatives from the affected states met. The meeting was originally called the "Meeting of Commissions to Remedy Defects of the Federal Government," and it was later called the Annapolis Convention, named for the city in which it took place.

Only twelve delegates from five states showed up, one of whom was Alexander Hamilton. At that convention, it was determined that more decisive action must take place in order to resolve the problems, which now were of national importance. It was decided, therefore, that a serious rewrite of the Articles of Confederation was needed.

The Battle for State Recognition: Vermont vs. New York

The Confederation Congress was now meeting in order to rewrite the Articles of Confederation, and the people who considered themselves citizens of the "Vermont Republic" wanted representation at the convention. That area was originally designated as either a part of the state of New Hampshire or of New York in a disputed area called the New Hampshire Grants. But that was back in the year 1764, prior to the Revolution. There was a group of protesters in that territory who objected to those classifications called the "Green Mountain Boys," who were led by a dynamic man called Ethan Allen. After the war, the people who lived there didn't want to be a part of either New York or New Hampshire. They wanted to instead form a separate state called Vermont. During 1777, "Vermont" applied for statehood but was repeatedly denied, even though they had their own state government in place. New York insisted that Vermont was a part of New York, but Vermont vehemently objected. Then New York Governor George Clinton took the extraordinary measure of asking Congress to declare war on "Vermont." Congress was aghast at this and rendered no decision on the matter.

Alexander Hamilton, as a well-respected New Yorker, realized that it was up to him to step in and restore the peace so that the convention could go about its job of formulating a new constitution. Toward that end, Hamilton contacted their representative lawyer, Nathaniel Chipman, and they both agreed that Vermont merited the status of a separate state. However, such a change would be time-consuming, as New York was reluctant to give up some of its landholdings there.

Kentucky was also having similar difficulties, as the neighboring state of Virginia was trying to claim it as part of their state. Kentucky argued that they were recognized as "Kentucky" under the prior Articles of Confederation but had been dropped as a recognized state for this new Confederation Congress.

In 1788, Hamilton wrote that these matters should be the first order of business under the new constitution: "One of the first subjects of deliberations with the new congress will be the independence of Kentucky for which the southern states will be anxious. The northern will be glad to find a counterpoise in Vermont."

The entire matter was finally settled when New York gave up its claim on Vermont and resolved their fiscal encumbrances. Vermont and New York eventually ironed out their difficulties, but Vermont wasn't recognized as a state until 1791, after the Constitutional Convention. In 1792, Kentucky was granted statehood.

Constitutional Convention

In 1787, representatives of the states were elected to attend the Constitutional Convention that was to be held in Philadelphia between 1787 and 1789. George Washington was the undisputed president of the convention, and Alexander Hamilton was the delegate from New York. Hamilton had a preference for a strong central government, not unlike that of Great Britain. Therefore, he made a speech early in the convention supporting what was later called a "President-for-Life." He made this proposal as he wanted the U.S. president to establish policies without having to be concerned about his own reelection. As a safeguard, he suggested that a president could be dismissed for what he termed "bad behavior." He said, "The supreme Executive authority of the United States to be vested in a Governor to be elected to serve during good behavior—the election to be made by Electors chosen by the people in the Election Districts."

Hamilton also recommended that some privileges be added to the executive branch: 1) veto power; 2) responsibility to direct a war effort, but the Senate alone would have the power to declare war; 3) the power to make treaties approved by the Senate; 4) the appointment of officials for departments of war, foreign affairs, and finance, and 5) the ability to pardon crimes except that of treason.

Hamilton's vision was to have a legislative division consisting of a Senate and a house assembly. Senators would be elected for life, while house members would be elected periodically.

For the judicial department, Hamilton supported a life-term for the justices, provided they demonstrated what he called again "good behavior."

The members of the Constitutional Convention were surprised at Hamilton's proposal that a president should serve for life, and they called Hamilton's proposal the "British plan." One of the other delegates, James Madison, felt that Hamilton was a sympathizer of a monarchical structure of government.

Members of the convention deviated from Hamilton's British plan in terms of the role of the chief executive. However, they agreed with him in terms of a tripartite division; that is, that the government should be divided into three branches—the executive, the legislative, and the judicial. They also differed with his view that senators should be appointed for life.

It was further determined that an executive branch should handle the implementation of laws passed by Congress, the power to veto a law—unless two-thirds of Congress approves it—sign treaties with other nations, and the power to grant pardons to those convicted of federal crimes. It was to be supported by four heads of cabinets: 1) Secretary of the Treasury; 2) Secretary of State; 3) Secretary of War; and 4) Attorney General.

The legislative branch, or Congress, would be bicameral, that is divided into two: the House of Representatives and the Senate. Laws would be proposed, discussed, and debated by the House and then by the Senate. If the piece of legislation had sufficient support, it was to be passed along to the Senate for debate and voted upon.

Congress was to have the right to tax the citizens. In addition, Congress would establish an annual budget for the country and have the power to declare war. The Senate, not the House of Representatives, however, was to have the ability to ratify treaties with other countries.

The judicial department would interpret the application of laws to particular situations. Juries would be appointed by the courts unless the defendant waived that right. The juries would then decide the guilt or innocence of the defendant, and the judge would pass sentence. If a jury trial was waived, the judge was to decide the case instead.

Although Hamilton had some reservations regarding the document in its final form, he far preferred this to the weaker Articles of Confederation and urged the people of New York to sign for ratification. The Constitution was then circulated among all the states for ratification, and it was ratified on June 21st, 1788.

Most of the people were expecting a modification of the Articles of Confederation, but this was a new and very different document from what the people expected.

The Federalist Papers

In order to shore up support from the states for the passage of the new Constitution, Alexander Hamilton, John Jay, and James Madison wrote 85 essays known as *The Federalist Papers*. Hamilton wrote under the pseudonym "Publius," a name he had used before. They were published in the largest newspapers in the region, including the *Independent Journal* and *The Daily Adviser*, in October 1787, and they were constantly reprinted in newspapers throughout the colonies for the rest of the year. In January 1788, they were published in book form, and it was titled *The Federalist: A Collection of Essays, Written in Favour of the New Constitution, as Agreed upon by the Federal Convention, September 17, 1787*.

After Hamilton died, a list came out, saying that Hamilton had written two-thirds of the essays alone. However, scholars now believe that some of those essays were indeed written by James Madison. This doesn't mean that Hamilton's contributions were lessened in any way. Hamilton wrote an astounding 51 articles, while James Madison wrote 29 and John Jay wrote only 5.

Some of the most influential essays that Hamilton wrote include Federalist No. 70, where Hamilton states that the country needs one chief executive, and Federalist No. 78, where he lays the groundwork for the idea of judicial review by the federal courts. In

Federalist No. 6, Hamilton warns against competition among the states and says that men "have in too many instances abused the confidence they possessed; and assuming the pretext of some public motive, have not scrupled to sacrifice the national tranquility to personal advantage or personal gratification." In Federalist No. 34, Hamilton spells out the kinds of questions citizens should consider concerning taxes. "Suppose then the convention had been inclined to proceed upon the principle of repartition of the objects of revenue, between the Union and its members in PROPORTION to their comparative necessities; what particular fund could have been selected for the use of the States, that would not either have been too much or too little for their present, too much for their future wants?"

There were incessant arguments among the people about the general structure of this new government. People split into two groups: the Federalists and the Anti-Federalists. The Federalists were those who envisioned a strong central government, while the Anti-Federalists felt that a strong central government would squelch the rights of individual states. Violent written rebuttals full of hyperboles raced back and forth in the press. Each side painted nightmare scenarios of what would happen if the other side was to prevail.

When the governor of New York, George Clinton, read the Constitution, he called it "a monster with open mouth and monstrous teeth ready to devour all before it" and scribbled off his own pieces under the pseudonym "Cato." He had firm objections against a stronger central government. Patrick Henry of the former Massachusetts Minutemen characterized it as "the tyranny of Philadelphia," and he even drew a comparison between the document and the "tyranny of George III." Hamilton, in particular, was hit with personal criticisms by those who knew he had used the pen name "Publius." These comments alluded to the fact that he was illegitimate and foreign-born. Knowing from whence the barbs were flung (Governor Clinton and his supporters), Hamilton handled it more objectively. It isn't known whether or not Clinton's supporters realized this was Hamilton's contribution, but he addressed the wider issues of international relations, and—in defense of the Constitution—he reminded his readers to note the series of checks and balances in this type of republication government not found in other political systems.

The First Election

New York City was considered the first capital of the United States. George Washington was elected as the first president of the country, as was expected, and John Adams was the vice president. For his Attorney General, he chose Edmund Randolph, who had served during the Constitutional Convention; for his Secretary of War, he chose Henry Knox, whose performance during the French and Indian War was excellent; for his Secretary of State, he chose Thomas Jefferson, who was excellent at foreign relations; and for his Secretary of the Treasury, he chose Alexander Hamilton, whose financial skills were known to him from his service as his aide-de-camp.

Washington wanted his Cabinet to be a group of people who had different ideas about governance. He liked the interchange of various ideas, hoping that one member might present the same issue from a different viewpoint.

Washington was an adept judge of personality and realized that there would be distinct differences between his fellow Virginian, Jefferson and the New Yorker Hamilton. Hamilton felt very strongly about the priority of national rights over states' rights in particular instances. However, Washington hoped that these two intellectuals might find some common ground between their two viewpoints that would satisfy most of the states. Washington also had the ability to understand their different political philosophies and lead them toward a compromise. Unfortunately, both were incredibly stubborn, and that never happened. They both became bitter political rivals over the sovereignty of states' rights and national rights, and neither one seemed to be able to compromise.

The Foreign War Debt Crisis

Not only were the Revolutionary War veterans owed money, but the foreign governments from whom America borrowed money were demanding payments. America's ambassador to England, John Adams, was placed in a very difficult position when he served there. Because the Articles of Confederation didn't allow a national government to enforce procedures for the collection of war debts, his only resource was to approach Congress and "ask" that they contribute funds. In addition, England had failed to remove some of its forts from northern New York through the terms of the Treaty of Paris. Adams had little power to have his own militia dismantle the forts. The heads of the British garrisons indicated that they would do so once the Americans had released the British property seized during the war.

Adams, as an ambassador, had also secured loans from wealthy Dutch bankers, but the federal government, again, had no financial machinery in place to satisfy these loans either. Likewise, the French government took enormous risks of both money and men to help America become independent.

Chapter 4 – Economy and the First National Bank

Hamilton and the Debt Crisis

One of America's first orders of business had to do with the procedures for paying its debt through its newly established Department of the Treasury under Alexander Hamilton. He called for the input of James Madison and Thomas Jefferson to tackle that issue. The country owed about 54 million dollars, and the states owed about 25 million. Hamilton expressed that concern very explicitly in his first report on public credit. He said:

> That exigencies are expected to occur in the affairs of nations in which there will be a necessity for borrowing. The loans in times of public danger especially from foreign war, are found an indispensable resource, even to the wealthiest of them. And that, in a country such as this, is possessed of little active wealth, or in other words, little moneyed capital, the necessity for that resource in such emergencies be proportionally urgent.

After the U.S. Constitution came into effect on March 4th, 1789, the new government had the authority to raise revenues through taxation. Through the Treasury Department, Hamilton had the freedom to charge a lower interest rate on land. Starting in 1790, he made regular payments to the French government. However, the total expenses incurred by the U.S. government exceeded the amount of money in the U.S. Treasury, so Hamilton sought out private loans through Dutch bankers. That helped to some extent, but money was still owed to the French. James Swan, an American banker, stepped in to assist and visited France to negotiate a settlement. He bought up the American loans, then turned around and sold those loans to others in exchange for a higher interest rate on the repayments. Americans and even the British, although unknowingly, bought shares in these securities. He did well with those, and the debts were finally being repaid.

The First Report on Public Credit

In January of 1790, Hamilton presented a three-part provision for paying back their debt using government bonds:

> 1. The foreign debt must be paid in full per the treaties.

> 2. The principal amount of the loan would be paid. Interest rates of four percent would be paid on short-term bonds; six percent interest would be paid for long-term bonds.

> 3. State debts would be assumed by the federal government, and interest wouldn't be due until 1792.

During the course of the war, federal certificates had been sold at a percentage of their stated value in order to raise capital rapidly. James Madison, whom Hamilton thought would support the provision, vehemently objected. Because the principal was to be paid in full plus interest, this would provide a windfall profit for those— mostly the wealthy Northerners—who had the resources to invest in the certificates. That would discriminate against those of lesser means who weren't able to purchase these certificates, like farmers, Madison said.

Hamilton felt that it was vital to pay state debts at their full price because some of the states had already been paid while others hadn't. The plans to repay the loans still owed to the federal government by some states were designed in such a way that the tax burdens would be evenly spread over the states for the next three years. The difficulty with this was the fact that it would be a logistical nightmare tracking down those individuals within the states that should be paid more. Hamilton admitted that there would be some inequalities, but he felt that those who received more money would reinvest it in the country. This is what is known today as the "trickle-down" theory.

The debate continued in Congress for months. In addition, the press issued bitter criticisms toward Hamilton, calling his plan the "bastard of eastern speculators." After a great deal of time had passed and it was ascertained that there weren't enough sufficient votes in Congress to get a bill passed, Jefferson asked that Madison and Hamilton sit down to a dinner meeting to hash it out. As most of the opposition resided in Virginia, Madison and Jefferson felt they could muster the sufficient votes needed to pass a bill if Hamilton would agree to move the country's capital near the Potomac River, which was around the halfway mark between the North and the South. Hamilton agreed, indicating that this transition from Philadelphia, which was the current U.S. capital, needed to be gradual in order to assuage the concerns of the public in and around Philadelphia.

The now-famous "dinner deal" was the last time that Alexander Hamilton, Thomas Jefferson, and James Madison would work together and emerge in a "win-win" situation.

The Second Report on Public Credit and the National Bank

In December of 1790, Hamilton indicated that, in order to handle these transactions, a national bank should be established. Madison and Jefferson, among others, objected to the establishment of the bank on the grounds that is was unconstitutional, and Washington was hesitant about it as well. Hamilton, however, argued that the government should not refuse to do for a nation what they could do for a person. There were private banks and corporations in the states run by individuals and boards of directors. In addition, this bank would not be an agency of the government, and Hamilton indicated that a government was, by its nature, sovereign.

Southerners like Madison and Jefferson simply didn't trust banks. First of all, such a bank would have special privileges that private banks didn't have, and it would diminish the importance of state banks who kept the smaller investors in mind. Secondly, this bank would be more of a profit-making vehicle for the wealthy who had more to invest, and they were more likely to invest their money in manufacturing than farming. Thirdly, this bank would be run by the wealthier investors who would cater to the needs of their friends more than the common good, and there was nothing in the Constitution giving the federal government the right to establish a bank in the first place.

Usually, banking and finance were handled by the Northerners, and the trust level between the North and the South was shaky. In order to include the contribution from the South, Hamilton stressed that fact that the United States, up until this point, had been too dependent upon imports from Britain and Europe in general. To balance that off, he encouraged the agricultural market to produce more crops and ship some overseas. In addition, they levied tariffs on imports from Great Britain and other countries. To stimulate new businesses, Hamilton also subsidized some new industries. Washington was convinced by Hamilton's arguments and signed the Funding Act of 1791. The bank was also chartered in that year and was set to expire in 1811. The First Bank of the United States was built in Philadelphia.

Initial Steps Toward Capitalization

To start the bank off on a good footing, custom houses were set up for the collection of tariffs owed by foreign shippers under the Customs Bureau, which had been established in 1789. During the

Revolutionary War, smuggling was common. Therefore, shipping routes and smuggler networks were already in place, so they simply fired up once again. In order to prevent the non-payment of tariffs, the country used the Revenue Cutter Service, which had been active during the war. As part of the Funding Act of 1790, those ships were armed, and arrangements were made to build more. It was their function to guard the eastern shore of the United States, enforce the tariffs, curtail piracy, and later on prevent the slave trade from reaching the country's shores when it was prohibited in early 1808. In addition, they could transport government officials and even carry the mail. Ben Franklin had already been the Postmaster General in 1753, and he was made responsible for creating and regulating mail delivery, utilizing the Revenue Cutters. In 1792, the Post Office Department was created. Postal inspections were systematized, and their function was to prevent the smuggling of contraband and other abuses. The Revenue Cutter Service later evolved into today's U.S. Coast Guard.

In 1784, 1785, and 1787, Northwest Ordinances were passed, granting ownership of unsettled lands west of the Mississippi River in order to expand the area of the United States. Those territories were wide and open ranges. However, they eventually wanted to apply for statehood in order to have all the rights and protections provided by the federal government. Part of the process for achieving statehood was to have the government sell plots of land. That resulted in monetary resources for the federal treasury, although it wasn't enough to pay off the country's foreign debt.

Hamilton's goal, like that of all Americans, was to be self-sufficient enough to buy and sell among the states, as well as to promote a healthy export business. Unlike Jefferson and Madison, George Washington didn't feel that the country was destined to be primarily an agricultural society. In 1789, Washington chided Congress, saying that free people should "promote such manufactories as tend to render them independent of others for essential." Congress asked Hamilton to prepare a report on the state of manufacturing in the country in order to make plans to establish a more independent economy.

The U.S. Mint

The First Bank of the United States had issued U.S. paper currency, but people were using the Spanish peso in addition. Hamilton felt that the United States should also have its own coinage. Therefore, in 1792, the Coinage Act was passed. It was the first building to be built under the Constitution, and its first coins were the ten-dollar gold Silver Eagle coin and the silver dollar. Coinage for less than that was created in denominations from a half-penny to fifty cents.

The Beginning of Industry

Hamilton wanted America to develop its own industries and manufacture truly American products, not only to pay off the war debts but to support the American people who lived within the country. In fact, the population was steadily increasing, and the administration needed to see to it that their economic needs were met.

In 1790, Alexander Hamilton appointed Tench Coxe, an economist and merchandizer, as the Assistant Secretary of the Treasury. Coxe had served as a delegate at the Continental Congress from 1788 to 1789. During the course of his mercantile experiences in England, Coxe indicated that the textile industry in England was superior to that in America. Interested in the industrial improvements that England possessed, they hired a man, Andrew Mitchell, to check out textile-making devices that were used over there. Mitchell made sketches of the machinery he was able to observe and passed them along to America.

While there, Mitchell discovered a British weaver named George Parkinson, who worked with an invention created by Richard Arkwright of Lancashire. He had created a device called a "spinning frame," which—when combined with horsepower, hydropower, and, later, a steam engine—could convert cotton to something called "cotton lap," a precursor in the yarn-making process. After improvements to his unit, Arkwright received a patent for another one of the units used in the process, a card-making machine. It was capable of producing long skeins of yarn suitable for weaving and crocheting. With a combination of those machines, Arkwright opened up cotton mills in Great Britain. In March of 1791, the U.S. government awarded a patent to Parkinson for his design for a flax mill, even though the affair had a tint of industrial espionage. There were, though, differences between Arkwright's designs and Parkinson's.

After that, Tench Coxe established the "Society for Establishing Useful Manufactures or S.E.U.M." The society envisioned creating automatic processes for the manufacture of other goods, such as women's shoes, stockings, hats, carpets, and the like. William Duer along with three other financiers of the society, Alexander Macomb, John Dewhurst, and Royal Flint, were also major investors in the First National Bank.

Hamilton helped Coxe write the prospectus for the society to help distribute to potential investors. An initial stock offering was made, and it was an enormous revenue-raising measure to help the burgeoning company. The capitalization of the company would come in part from the purchase of government bonds. They selected a site near the Passaic Falls in New Jersey, which could be used to supply the hydropower needed to operate the machinery. Hamilton then showed it to Governor William Paterson, who was very excited about the profit this would bring into his state. In his honor, the city for the site of the plant was called Paterson. From that point on, Paterson grew as an industrial city.

Report on Manufactures

In 1791, Hamilton indicated that America was, in effect, isolated from the rest of the world in terms of commerce. Manufacturing needed to be set up like that of the Passaic Falls project. In fact, once other manufacturers and merchants heard about the industrial plan, they wanted to emigrate to the United States. To them, it was a land of opportunity and new untapped markets.

Hamilton figured that the addition of moderate tariffs for imported goods could raise revenue without threatening the growth of home industries. A portion of those tariffs, he reasoned, could be used to provide subsidies for start-up companies. Given a sufficient profit from tariffs, that money could be targeted to build roads and canals.

There was, as might be predicted, a great deal of opposition to this report. Most of the country had, up until 1790, been agrarian-based. James Madison, in particular, objected to the preference given to those involved in manufacturing unless it was handled properly. He feared that corruption and favoritism would enter the system because politicians might be unduly influenced. The farming community had no subsidies, and many felt that put them at a distinct disadvantage. Today, however, that situation is reversed because farming is subsidized, mostly due to the cost of land in the agrarian sector and unpredictable weather.

Eventually, Congress adopted most of Hamilton's policies in this report because of the protective nature of tariffs. However, it remained a bone of contention between the North and the South up until the Civil War (1861 to 1865.)

Dawn of the Political Parties

The delegates of the Constitutional Convention differed significantly on one issue—that concerning the amount of power granted to the executive branch and the power granted to Congress. The Articles of Confederation had been scrapped due to the fact that nearly all of the power rested in the hands of the states, leaving the executives with virtually little. The president, therefore, couldn't make treaties, charge tariffs, or the like. Once the Constitution was ratified, the central administration held more power, but it was balanced off with checks and balances due to things like congressional vetoes.

The two parties at the time were the Federalists, who sought to have a strong government and weaker state governments, and the Anti-Federalists, who preferred that more power be held by the states than the central government. In time, with the rise of Thomas Jefferson, a wider party platform was developed. He and James Madison formed what was called the Republican Party, although historians refer to it as the Democratic-Republican Party or the Jeffersonian Republican Party to differentiate it from the Republican Party today. It opposed the centralizing feature of the strong national government that the Federalists believed in, and they believed that the states should have more power and a greater say in the functions of the federal government. This party began around the year 1792.

The Democratic-Republican Party could be viewed as a counterreaction to the policies of Alexander Hamilton. Men like Thomas Jefferson saw in Hamilton an imitation of the British style of government, and they feared that a system such as that could lead the nation back to a despotic tyranny that was so typical of Europe. Not to be overlooked is the fact that an agrarian economy and a manufacturing economy differed in many ways. Both Jefferson and Madison came from an agrarian background and had experienced the manipulations of financial networks that could deleteriously harm the everyday man who was limited by economic conditions, environment, climatic conditions, and other forces of nature over which he had little control. It wasn't until later that factors entered in to limit the power of the manufacturing sector, like global competition, prices on world markets, foreign wars, and international political conditions.

Today, the best corollary for the evolution of the United States political parties might be said in this way: The Federalists of today are now Republicans, and the Democratic-Republicans are today's Democrats.

Chapter 5 – The Time the Troubles Start

The Early Banks

The first bank established in the United States was the Bank of North America in 1781. The Continental Congress chartered it, and the first shareholders were Ben Franklin, Thomas Jefferson, and Alexander Hamilton. It offered the high interest rate of fourteen percent on its dividends. Boston opened the Massachusetts Bank in 1784. New York petitioned for another bank to service its many customers and opened the Bank of New York in 1784. It wasn't entirely capitalized, so it wasn't chartered at that time. The first shareholders were William Seton, Alexander McDougall, Alexander Hamilton, and Aaron Burr.

The Banking Prejudice and Aaron Burr

Hamilton wrote the charter for the Bank of New York in 1791. The Bank of New York, a private bank, was generally quite successful but was discriminatory. What it failed to do was loan money to those who were followers of Thomas Jefferson and the Democratic-Republicans. All the banks were run by the Federalists until Aaron

Burr came along. Burr was a Revolutionary War veteran who later became a lawyer and then a senator in 1791 after having defeated Philip Schuyler, Hamilton's father-in-law. Burr was a Democratic-Republican and a big player in the political power complex in New York, especially after gaining the support of George Clinton. It is curious to note that Burr lived just a block away from Alexander Hamilton.

Burr was determined to forge his way into banking so that the Democratic-Republicans could have a foothold in it. In an insightful but rather devious proposal, Burr indicated that a source of fresh water was needed for the city of New York and worked with Alexander Hamilton, William Seton, and three other Federalists in a bipartisan effort to accomplish that through what was called the Manhattan Water Company. The bill was passed into law by the New York Congress.

However, the Manhattan Water Company was just a puppet company and pumped very little water. When its charter was written, Burr managed to cleverly sneak in a clause "to employ surplus capital in any moneyed transactions or operations not inconsistent with the and constitution of this state or of the United States." That allowed the water company itself to not only take deposits but make loans. Those loans were open to the Democratic-Republicans and represented a major change in the banking industry. Now, the Federalists no longer had a monopoly on loans. Eventually, the Manhattan Water Company merged with Chase National Bank to form the Chase Manhattan Bank, which was one of the earliest institutions that formed the current J.P. Morgan Chase company.

The Bank Panic of 1792

The price of the securities in the First National Bank rose quickly, as investors were interested in the purchase of the government-backed bonds. However, in the spring of 1792, the price of the securities suddenly started to fall. Investors panicked, and as they did so, more investors pulled out. When the prices of the securities were falling,

Hamilton wrote to William Duer of the Society for the Establishing of Useful Manufactures, saying, "I trust they (the funds) are not diverted. The public interest and my reputation are deeply concerned in this matter." As a matter of fact, Duer had taken thousands of dollars from the society's funds, so all of that money was now missing. John Dewhurst, another investor, had taken 50,000 dollars for a loan to purchase textile equipment, but he absconded with the money. That problem dovetailed into one of their own creation. The two men had concocted a scheme to take out loans from elsewhere and get a minor monopoly on selling securities. When the prices of the securities fell, Duer couldn't make his payments; neither could Malcomb, and—of course—Dewhurst was among the missing. Both Duer and Malcomb were imprisoned. Dewhurst went bankrupt and fled to England where he continued with his manipulative speculating.

Hamilton used some of his own money and got a loan from William Seton of the Bank of New York to help resolve the crisis within the S.E.U.M. Because of that, the S.E.U.M. was able to offer some of its programs in Paterson.

As for the national bank crisis, it was exacerbated by a parallel crisis in the Bank of New York. Hamilton again approached his friend, William Seton, asking that he purchase more of the public debt. However, because of all those requests, the Bank of New York was overextended. New speculators also thought they had a new source of revenue in this bank, but the bank had to curtail back, as they had little left in reserve. While it didn't fail to make the periodic payments to the securities investors, the Bank of New York couldn't renew its 30-day loans, so investors had to go elsewhere. They were then forced to sell their securities, but the prices fell drastically.

In March of 1792, the National Bank resorted to what was called the "Sinking Fund Commission," which was composed of Vice President John Adams, Attorney General Edmund Randolph, Secretary of State Thomas Jefferson, and Chief Justice John Jay. Hamilton proposed that the national securities be put on the open markets. They needed a majority vote, but John Jay was away. They voted on the measure anyway, but the vote was half for and half against. After much discussion, however, Randolph was persuaded to change sides, and the measure was passed. Hamilton also guaranteed that the government would buy up to 500,000 dollars of securities in case the National Bank was stymied by too much collateral.

In a series of contracts with William Seton of the Bank of New York, they offered him bank loans collateralized by national debt securities at a higher interest rate—seven percent. In addition, they guaranteed to have 150,000 dollars available in open-market loans. The crisis was successfully averted, and the financial conditions reverted back to normal.

The Whiskey Rebellion

There was no income tax in 1790. However, to help make up the shortfall in paying war debt, Hamilton proposed to the Congress that a tax be charged on domestically produced spirits and whiskey. Because it was considered a luxury rather than a necessity, he felt it would have little reaction. He was wrong. Farmers in western Pennsylvania, in particular, rose up in a rebellion which lasted until 1794. Nearly all of the farmers had whiskey stills, as the alcohol could be made from the byproducts of the grain they harvested. It could also be made from corn, wheat, and barley—all of which the farmers grew in abundance. After hearing the practical complaints, Hamilton reduced the amount charged. However, he gave the larger distilleries more of an advantage, as it took more money to operate them safely and produce a high-quality product. Every still had to be registered, which was a hardship on the smaller manufacturers. Inspectors and tax collectors arrived at these establishments, infuriating the distillers. It reminded them of the times when the British inspectors canvassed their towns in search of customs and duties.

Resistance and harassment of these excise tax collectors were rampant. Some of the men's homes were broken into and ransacked. Collectors were tarred, feathered, and marched in the streets. Writs (which are like warrants) were written liberally against those who refused to pay the excise tax. William Findley, who was one of the congressional officials from Pennsylvania, had the law made to be more practical by requiring that the smaller offenders be heard in local courts rather than traveling miles and miles to Philadelphia. He objected to many of Hamilton's more stringent measures, which he felt would do harm to the smaller farmers. Many historians indicate that Hamilton's heavy-handed approached triggered some of the violence that followed.

The rest of the government writs were given to the parties concerned without incident, but it didn't stop there. In July 1794, Federal Marshal David Lenox, who was joined by General John Neville, made his rounds around western Pennsylvania until they were shot at by the men who were holed up at Miller's farm. The next day, at least thirty men surrounded Neville's home, and they demanded the surrender of the federal marshal, who they believed to be inside; he actually went home following the events the previous day. Neville responded to their demands by firing a shot that killed one of the men outside. They opened fire but were unable to dislodge Neville. So, they came back the next day, this time with nearly 600 men. Ten U.S. Army soldiers also arrived to aid Neville in the fight. Following negotiations that went nowhere, the women and the children were released unharmed before both sides began shooting. Some died in the crossfire, including Major James McFarlane, a veteran of the Revolutionary War who sided with the rebels. McFarlane was given the funeral of a hero, but that only served to arouse the hatreds manifested between the two opposing forces.

Rumors then proliferated that crops, too, would be taxed. Farmers in those areas started to feel that this would result in a repeat of the excessive taxation levied by Great Britain during the Revolutionary War. An uprising occurred in Hagerstown, Maryland, over this issue.

The people rushed to their armories and took weapons and ammunition to prepare for an imagined incursion from the national government, forcing as many able-bodied men to join them as possible. Washington reviewed his troops at Fort Cumberland, Maryland, and put "Light-Horse Harry" Lee in charge. They met with little resistance, and the crowds disbursed.

George Washington himself donned his military uniform and led an army of nearly 12,000 men to western Pennsylvania. The formidable size of his force was sufficient enough to disperse the rebels.

Washington's Watermelon Army

After the uprising at Miller's farm, Washington explored western Pennsylvania further. He marched at the head of what was called a "Watermelon Army." The Watermelon Army may have had the appearance and the abilities of an army, but its function belied its appearance. Washington took the opportunity to march through these rural areas in Pennsylvania, Maryland, and Virginia to admire the appearance of the various villages and towns and praise the progress they had made since the devastation of the Revolutionary War battles fought on their land. These people weren't rebels, he noted; they were hard-working, patriotic Americans working together to build a society. From time to time, he stopped and met with the community spokesmen, asking them about their grievances and their hopes and plans for the future. Washington took his time talking to them, and he stayed in many of their farmhouses.

This trip had two results: 1) It showed the population that the national government had the power and strength to quell insurrections, and 2) the national government had the ability to listen to and respond to the needs of the common people who lived in the states.

Outcome

Many of the rebels involved in the insurrection disappeared westward into the mountains. Only two were captured—Philip

Wiggle and John Mitchell, one of whom had assaulted a tax collector and the other whom burned down a house. Although they were sentenced to death by hanging, Washington pardoned them. He was desperately trying to keep the country united. The tax on domestic whiskey was later rescinded under the following presidential administration—that of Thomas Jefferson—in 1801.

Crisis of Another Sort

Hamilton was a feverish worker, but he could be jovial and charming at the social events he attended. Often, he and his wife, Eliza, were entertained by Martha and George Washington. Hamilton liked arriving late at parties, relishing the attention he received when he did so. Most people found him very pleasant and agreeable. When he spoke, everyone tended to stop speaking so as to catch his every word. The ladies were especially fascinated by his charm and grace.

His graciousness and generosity got him into trouble in 1791. As he often traversed the walkways of the city of Philadelphia, he came across many admirers. Hamilton was a good-looking man with a calm demeanor, so people felt comfortable approaching him. One day, a demure woman by the name of Maria Reynolds walked up to him and asked that he visit her in her boarding house where she might discuss an urgent matter with him privately. Foolishly, he met her there. Maria then asked him for some help because her husband had abandoned her. Did he perhaps have some money he could spare so she could take care of herself? He agreed, excused himself, and later returned with some money for her. Maria cried about the vulgarity of her husband, James. Then she added that she still truly loved her husband but that her distress over the abuse was overwhelming. Hamilton felt pity for her, and perhaps that only added to his attraction to her. The two of them began having intimate relations with each other, and his affair with her only escalated over the weeks. They frequently met during the summer and fall to continue in the wild and torrid relationship.

In truth, Maria had a local reputation for engaging in prostitution, although Hamilton didn't know that. The neighbors said that Maria's husband was well aware of Maria's promiscuity and of Hamilton's relationship with her. James Reynolds knew full well that Hamilton stood to lose a lot should the affair be made public, so he seized the opportunity and insisted on 1,000 dollars in December to keep the matter private. Hamilton paid the money and ended his relationship with Maria. However, Reynolds wrote Hamilton in January 1792 to invite him to visit his wife again. Maria, who might have been manipulated into the scheme by her husband, began to write and seduce Hamilton whenever she knew her husband would be away, and it was too much for Hamilton to resist. After these visits, Hamilton would send thirty or forty dollars. The last payment he sent was in June 1792, which might have been the end of the affair.

In November 1792, Reynolds was imprisoned for counterfeiting and speculating on veterans' back pay, and he wrote to Hamilton for assistance. However, Hamilton refused to help, and not even Maria's letters would sway him otherwise this time. James Reynolds' accomplice, Jacob Clingman, who had also been imprisoned, informed some of Hamilton's rivals that Reynolds had information they could use against their political opponent. James Monroe, a Virginia statesman, Frederick Muhlenberg, the speaker of the House of Representatives, and Abraham Venable, a representative from Virginia, visited Reynolds in jail, who only hinted at Hamilton's misconduct before disappearing after his release from jail. However, the three men believed that Hamilton was involved in the crime Reynolds and Clingman were charged with, not that he was involved in an affair. They even visited Maria, who confirmed their suspicions that Hamilton was involved in speculation, giving them some of his notes that he sent.

Instead of immediately making the matter public, Monroe and the others decided to confront Hamilton directly. Hamilton then revealed the actual truth to them and gave them the letters from the Reynolds'. The three men were satisfied with Hamilton's explanation and decided to keep the matter private. However, Monroe did retain copies of the Reynolds' letters and sent them to Thomas Jefferson, Hamilton's perennial nemesis. Jefferson held on to those letters until later on.

The harm that could have been caused by that episode loomed large in Hamilton's mind, and he spent years ruminating about it. In 1797, a muckraker by the name of James Callender obtained the notes from Monroe's committee about the Reynolds-Hamilton affair and wrote a series of pamphlets about it. Callender published them, adding his own embellishments to the story.

The Possible Duel: Hamilton vs. Monroe

After Hamilton left his post in the Department of the Treasury, the publicity about the Reynolds affair had deleteriously affected his public life. Hamilton suspected that the information about his affair had been released by James Monroe and met with him along with two witnesses, Hamilton's brother-in-law John Church and his friend, David Gelston, to discuss it. When confronted, James Monroe denied any knowledge about the release of the information regarding the committee investigation. The witnesses reported that Monroe leaped up and hollered at Hamilton, shouting, "Do you say I represented you falsely? You are a scoundrel!"

To that, Hamilton replied, "I will meet you like a gentleman."

"I am ready. Get your pistols," Monroe shouted.

The two witnesses, Church and Gelston, then stood between the two men until their sanity returned.

Monroe himself was highly agitated about Hamilton because he had been suddenly recalled from France by George Washington in 1796 where he had been an ambassador. George Washington had given him no reason for it either. Monroe felt that he was dismissed from his ambassadorship to France because of Hamilton's influence. That wasn't true at all, though. Monroe was recalled because Washington heard a rumor from Senator Gouverneur Morris that Monroe was stirring up anti-American sentiment in France. It also wasn't true that Monroe was stoking anti-American sentiment or that he had released information about the Reynolds-Hamilton affair to a muckraker. Monroe's secretary, James Beckley, had. Beckley was a clerk who had worked with Munroe and the other investigators, and he had made his own copies and handed them off to James Callender.

Despite being upset with Hamilton, Munroe promised him that he would get to the bottom of what happened and send him a full explanation of it. However, Hamilton was not appeased with the explanation he received a week later. He zeroed in on Munroe not refuting Clingman's charges of him misusing government money, a crime that was more serious to him than adultery. He demanded that Munroe refute them, which he declined to do. Things escalated again, and Munroe eventually told Hamilton that they could settle things in a way "which I am ever ready to meet." This could be seen as a veiled challenge of a duel.

Hamilton took it as such, and he accepted, saying that his second would visit to finalize the details. Monroe chose Burr to be his second, and it was Burr, oddly enough, the man that later killed Hamilton in a duel, that resolved the tensions between the two men. Burr delivered a letter to Hamilton from Munroe which stated that Munroe had misunderstood Hamilton's previous letter and denied issuing the challenge. However, perhaps so he didn't appear to be a coward, he told Hamilton that if he wished to fight that he should arrange it with Burr. Burr managed to convince the two to avoid it, saying they were being childish.

By mid-August, the two had settled down. However, Hamilton still felt that his reputation was still tarnished, so he decided to go public with the story. On August 25th, he printed the *Observations on Certain Documents*, later known as the Reynolds Pamphlet, where he admitted the entire affair but denied all charges of corruption.

Since Hamilton included his correspondence with Monroe in the pamphlet, Monroe wondered if things really were settled between the two. It is unknown how the drama between these two Founding Fathers settled itself as the two were still discussing the possibility of a duel in early 1798. Perhaps Hamilton was more interested in getting a new foothold in politics when relations between the United States and France heated up, causing him to forget about the petty squabble between himself and Monroe.

Chapter 6 – Empowerment of Political Parties

There are always groups and social centers within communities and countries that rise from a common root, like veterans' organizations, patriotic endeavors, hereditary groups, fundraising societies, and the like. Politics is no exception. Sometimes social clubs morph into political organizations. As these groups evolve, they often change focus or direction, depending upon the needs of the community.

The Society of the Cincinnati

The Society of the Cincinnati was a patriotic organization established, and it was composed of officers of the Continental Army and French soldiers who had participated in the American Revolution. It was originally formed during the Continental Army's encampment at Newburgh, New York, in 1783. Within ten years, members of the society were composed of many of the Founding Fathers like George Washington, General Henry Knox, and General von Steuben. The society held social events at which many of them conversed about political topics. Although George Washington himself declared no political party, most of the members of this society were Federalists. Originally, the society was based on a hereditary membership, but that requirement was later abolished. Alexander Hamilton succeeded George Washington as the society's president in 1784.

Most of the members were also wealthy, and many were landowners or involved in areas of advanced finances. Eventually, the society established state societies, where they often discussed matters involving the constitution and governance of their state. A large number of the members were from the northeastern states, and they exercised control of banks and industries. Prejudices arose as the state societies tended to favor their own members.

As the years progressed, this organization became more political.

The Tammany Society, Aka Tammany Hall

The Tammany Society used Native American terms to symbolize themselves as true or "pure" Americans. Early on, they declared themselves as a political entity. Although it had members from both political parties, the inclusion of the powerful George Clinton brought in representation from the Democratic-Republicans. By 1798, it became a political club of highly placed Democratic-Republicans. Its purpose was to create party unity on various issues and to support certain candidates for elections while opposing others. The Clinton family was one of the most powerful families in New York and controlled the Tammany Society for years. Hamilton spent a lot of energy enlisting the support of the ex-Loyalists and moderate former Whigs to wrest political control from the over-powerful Clinton faction. To this day, many cities, towns, and even streets in the tristate area bear the name of "Clinton." The society used the tactic of attracting the most recent immigrant population, making promises to them if their favorite candidates were elected. In time, the Tammany Society became very corrupt, exchanging political favors for money and/or lucrative positions in the local governments.

The Tammany Society primarily operated in New York. In the late 18th century, the Tammany Society met in an upper room of city hall that was often called "Tammany Hall." Although they moved their conference room to a Nassau Street tavern, the name stuck. Tammany Hall adopted the aim of countering the Federalist Party and their political candidates. Another ambitious politician, Aaron Burr, a Democratic-Republican, used the power of the Tammany Society to help him rise up in political circles. In 1789, Clinton was the governor of New York, and he appointed Aaron Burr as the state attorney general. Two years later, in 1791, Clinton was instrumental in getting Burr elected as a New York senator. Philip Schuyler, Alexander's father-in-law, served as a U.S. senator for the state of New York from 1789 to 1791, but due to the rising influence of Tammany Hall, he lost that election to Aaron Burr. Hamilton was furious and personally held that against Burr. In 1796, John Adams' wife, Abigail, who was quite astute about politics, told her husband that the Democratic-Republicans might have been considering Burr to run against Adams for the presidency.

Hamilton wasted no courtesies when he spoke about Burr. "He is for or against nothing, but as it suits his interest or ambition. He is determined as I conceive, to make his way to be the head of the popular party and in a word, to become like an "Embryo-Caesar" in the United States."

Jefferson vs. Hamilton

Hamilton was a strong and smart man. Despite the fact that he said he preferred the quiet life, he thrived on controversy and spent a great deal of his life involved in it. To Hamilton, engaging in the war between the political parties was like a game of tug-of-war. Jefferson also felt that way. In 1798, he said, "In every free and deliberating society, there must, from the nature of man, be opposite parties, violent dissension and discord; and one of these, for the most part, must prevail over the other for a longer or shorter time." According to Jefferson, the Federalists held the belief that "the executive branch of our government needs the most support." As for Jefferson's view of his own party, he said, "The republicans [Democratic-Republicans] compose the only form of government which is not eternally at open or secret war with the rights of mankind." Jefferson often defined his party not in terms of what it stood for but for what it didn't support.

When a national bank was proposed, Jefferson and Hamilton argued incessantly. Jefferson was vigorously opposed to banks under the auspices of a national government. Jefferson was a Southerner, and Southerners were often hurt by private bankers from the North, who would seize their farms if they defaulted on their loans. Hamilton, on the other hand, was more concerned about the status of America in the eyes of foreign countries, so he wanted to be sure that America gained the reputation for paying its loans and resolving its debt.

Since the Revolution, Great Britain had no ambassador in the United States. Hamilton felt it would be prudent to invite a British ambassador to the country and reopen communications between Britain and America for the economic advantage both would receive. Prior to the Revolution, there was a brisk trade between Britain and America that had slackened after the war. Because there was a common link between the two countries culturally, it would have been advantageous to exchange ambassadors. Hamilton's unofficial envoy to Great Britain, George Beckwith, agreed, saying, "We think in English and have a similarity of prejudices and of predilections." James Madison and Thomas Jefferson felt differently, however, and considered Britain to be corrupt and greedy. They preferred France as a major trading partner instead. Hamilton, on the other hand, harbored a deep antipathy for France and considered them "dangerous" because of the somewhat chaotic events going on in the country at the time. Although he had befriended Lafayette, Hamilton felt that close relations with France would be disastrous as it might trigger a trade war.

Madison favored tariffs levied against Great Britain based on tonnage, which would have made the fees higher. Both Madison and Jefferson cited the fact that Great Britain had yet to relinquish their forts on American soil, which was an agreement in the Treaty of Paris. In truth, however, America hadn't yet paid its war debt nor returned all the property belonging to British citizens in America, which is one reason the British held onto the forts.

Jefferson was the secretary of state at that time and should have been drawn more fully into this discussion about trade. However, he wasn't. Hamilton had already met with the unofficial British envoy, George Beckwith, in 1791 and later on covertly met with the official British ambassador, George Hammond, and groundwork was laid for trade relations. Hamilton had overstepped his bounds by manipulating foreign policy, which was the duty of Jefferson as the secretary of state, but Hamilton was concerned about too much involvement with France. As it turned out, that was a fortuitous occurrence because France was on the verge of bankruptcy in the late 1700s. The expenditures of the Wars of the Coalition and their financial aid to the United States during the American Revolutionary War had nearly exhausted the French treasury. In addition, the extravagant spending of the royal monarch, King Louis XVI, and his wife, Marie Antoinette, had cut further holes into the French economy.

Due to the economic trauma, the French people rebelled, deposing their king in 1792 and setting up a new government run by a mixed group of French militants that eventually evolved into the Legislative Assembly, which was headed up by a political faction called the Girondins and then later the Jacobins. Those who fell out of favor were executed on that frightening apparatus known as the guillotine during the Reign of Terror. King Louis XVI himself was even guillotined, along with his wife about nine months later. After that, France declared war on the British monarchy and was cheered on by Thomas Jefferson and other Democratic-Republicans. That support was short-lived. When that war spread to other monarchies in Europe, the situation became precarious for the United States.

George Washington wanted to declare neutrality, but the Treaty of Alliance and Amity signed after the Revolution required that

America ally itself with France. Washington met with his Cabinet. Hamilton reasoned that the treaty should not be adhered to if it was dangerous to other nations with whom America had relations. Secretary of War Henry Knox agreed. Thomas Jefferson and Edmund Randolph, however, supported the alliance with France. Jefferson and Hamilton engaged in a shouting match, and the argument continued until Washington put a stop to it. Washington then cast the determining vote and passed the Proclamation of Neutrality on April 22nd, 1793.

During that same year, a Frenchman by the name of Edmond Genêt had been seeking support for France during the Revolution and was already in the United States. He broke protocol and undermined Washington's Proclamation of Neutrality by failing to greet President Washington upon his arrival and purchasing some confiscated British ships for France. In addition, he recruited Americans to serve as privateers on those ships. Genêt had landed in South Carolina, and the South, in particular, favored France due to Jefferson's influence. He was even met with a parade!

Although Jefferson was pro-French, he was angry with Genêt over his political *faux pas*. So was Hamilton, and that was one of the few issues on which Jefferson and Hamilton agreed.

Genêt continued with his recruiting efforts and showed no sign of relenting. Washington then dispatched a letter to France demanding that Genêt be recalled. Genêt demanded that America make its periodic payments to pay back the war debt. Both Jefferson and Hamilton indicated that the payment should be delayed, although they disagreed as to how. Hamilton wanted to write a stern letter, but Jefferson wanted one that was more cordial. An argument, once again, ensued between the two of them. And again, Washington had to step in and decided to send the more polite version.

Totally exasperated by his dealings with Alexander Hamilton, Thomas Jefferson attempted to resign from his position as secretary of state. Washington persuaded him to hold off until the fall-out from the Genêt affair had passed. Jefferson ended up resigning on December 31st, 1793.

As for Genêt, he sailed for France. However, upon his arrival, he sadly discovered that his political supporters, the Girondins, were no longer in control. He feared for his safety, so, he turned around and sailed back for the United States. This time, he abided by the protocols, landing in Philadelphia, and he begged Washington to let him remain in the country. Washington granted his request. Genêt settled down and married the daughter of Governor George Clinton of New York. After that, Genêt faded into history.

The Jay Treaty of 1794

In 1793, when France and England were at war, George Washington consulted the members of his Cabinet, including Alexander Hamilton, concerning his wish to maintain neutrality. The United States was just in the process of establishing its own policies regarding internal taxation, the nature of the country's credit, and the status of the manufacturing sector. At that time, the country was in no position to fund a war, having fought a long and bloody war for independence on their own soil. Washington then sent Justice John Jay over to Great Britain to draw up a treaty of peace. This treaty placed Britain on a "most favored nation" status, which would give them preferential treatment for trade purposes and maintain neutrality simultaneously. Hamilton, it is said, penned most of the treaty for John Jay to carry over there, if it could be passed by Congress. Most of the members of Congress at that time were Federalists and roundly supported it. However, many of the Democratic-Republicans in Congress felt that some similar allowances should be given to France. Because the Federalists had the majority in Congress, though, it passed with the required two-thirds majority.

Unfortunately, it wasn't the most ideal of all treaties, giving rise to arguments in Congress and among the people. Not all points in the treaty were addressed, including those that required that the British close up their forts still on American soil. In addition, the impressment of American sailors still continued, compensation for merchant vessels confiscated during the war hadn't been made, and there was no compensation for kidnapped slaves.

Hamilton and Slavery

Hamilton had his own stance on the issue of slavery. He had seen the sufferings of the slaves on his home island of Saint Croix. He saw their squalor. At the firm of Kortright and Cruger, slaves were occasionally auctioned off, although that wasn't their major function. Hamilton was in charge of keeping order with the slaves but disliked that immensely. In 1777, he wrote critiques against the planters at Saint Croix using biblical language, saying, "O ye who revel in affluence see the afflictions of humanity and bestow your superfluity to ease them. Say not, we have suffered also, and thence withhold your compassion. What are your sufferings compared to those? Ye have still more than enough left. Act wisely. Succour the miserable and lay up a treasure in heaven."

In his writings, he often compared the condition of slavery to the manner in which Great Britain treated the American colonists. Through his church, he befriended Elias Boudinot, a Cherokee abolitionist, and that association led him to consider joining the Manumission Society after the Revolutionary War. Although Hamilton abhorred slavery, he placed his personal ambition ahead of taking any forceful actions to abolish the practice.

In 1779, Henry Laurens and Alexander Hamilton recommended to George Washington that he recruit African slaves to help in the war effort, telling him that they would make excellent soldiers. Hamilton also sent a letter to John Jay in that regard, saying, "The dictates of humanity and true policy equally interest me in favor of this unfortunate class of men." The army sent Hamilton and Laurens to South Carolina to recruit troops made from the slaves living there. Once there, they proposed to the legislature that they should raise these battalions, which the owners of the slaves would be given contributions. At the war's end, those who survived would be free men. Many of the Founding Fathers felt that blacks were inferior, but Hamilton, who had lived among them in the West Indies, never felt that way. After the war, Hamilton joined the Manumission Society in 1785, which supported freedom for the slaves. He served as its president briefly. Some of the other members were John Jay, Gouverneur Morris, and Rufus King. As president of the Manumission Society, Hamilton loudly protested about how citizens were circumventing state laws against slave sales by exporting slaves from other states. Oddly enough, however, the Manumission Society's administrators themselves owned slaves, and Hamilton attempted to remedy that but without success. Many of the leaders of the new nation felt that emancipation of slavery should be a gradual process, and Hamilton grudgingly signed bills in the new Constitution that supported that. He set his priority instead upon supporting bills that would strengthen the cohesiveness of the union.

Eliza's family owned slaves, and his mother-in-law willed her slaves to her. Neither she nor Alexander took possession of them, though. There was some evidence that Eliza sold them, however. During Hamilton's life, there was never any evidence that he himself owned any slaves.

Alexander Hamilton Resigns

Hamilton had become increasingly frustrated with his role as secretary of the treasury as the opposition to his policies increased. He also tended to stir up very strong feelings among Congress and other influential men in the community. Hamilton personally had a heavy-handed way of dealing with issues and was headstrong—a personality trait that worked to his disadvantage. At home, his wife had a miscarriage during the time when the Whiskey Rebellion was in progress, and he couldn't help comfort her when she needed him most. This sad event caused him to focus more on affairs at home. In addition, he was only receiving about 3,000 dollars for his services as the secretary of the treasury, and he knew he could make much more as a lawyer. That would help his family and help him feel better about himself. So, in the year 1795, he tendered his resignation to George Washington. Hamilton, however, fully intended to participate in politics but more as someone who operated behind the scenes.

A Possible Duel Between Alexander Hamilton and James Nicholson

James Nicholson, a retired naval officer with the Continental Army, became a Democratic-Republican during the rise of Thomas Jefferson. Nicholson also belonged to the Democratic Society of New York. In the year 1795, he was involved in a political debate over the Jay Treaty of 1794. Hamilton had apparently sent a proposed resolution to one of the committee meetings of the Democratic Society, "declaring it unnecessary to give an opinion on the treaty." The committee summarily rejected it, after which Hamilton later got into an argument with Josiah Hoffman, a Federalist lawyer, and James Nicholson, a member of the Democratic-Republicans. Not only that, but Nicholson accused Hamilton, via a friend of Hamilton's, of investing some of the U.S. Treasury funds into a British bank. The friend asked Nicholson for proof of this, and Nicholson indicated he could produce it if Hamilton attempted to run for public office. Hamilton then sent a letter to Nicholson demanding proof. Nicholson reiterated that there was proof and warned Hamilton that there might be consequences should this come to the public eye.

Letters flew back and forth between them, sometimes two per day. In one of the letters, Hamilton challenged Nicholson to meet him face-to-face at Paulus Hook. Paulus, today a section of Liberty State Park, is in Jersey City, and that area was often used for duels in the 18th century. As it turned out, DeWitt Clinton, among others, met with Nicholson with a draft of an apology letter for him to sign. The draft said, in part, "The subscribers (Clinton et. al.) having been made acquainted with the correspondence between Mr. Hamilton and Mr. Nicholson relative to a controversy that took place between them on Saturday before last, do hereby certify the same has been settled in a satisfactory and honorable way to both parties."

Washington's Retirement

In 1796, Washington longed to take refuge again in the private life sector, and he decided not to seek the office of the presidency for another term. Although he didn't publicly deliver it, Washington published it in the *American Daily Advertiser* after Alexander Hamilton helped to rewrite it. The initial draft of the address was written by James Madison when Washington first considered retirement. During 1796, the Genêt affair had had a profound effect on George Washington and was reflected in that address. Although it wasn't the only example, Genêt's attempt to prevail upon the liberty promulgated by America toward the end of the 18th century was extremely presumptuous and highlighted Washington's caution about foreign entanglements, which was one of the major themes of his speech. The second major theme had to do with political factions. He was emotionally exhausted by acting as a referee between Thomas Jefferson and Alexander Hamilton. Like Jefferson, Hamilton was very partisan, and—as a matter of fact—Washington had to modify Hamilton's draft of his farewell address quite a bit in order to remove some of its harsh wording.

Washington stressed the word "unity" in the address to give impetus to the commonly held core beliefs of all Americans, regardless of their political party. He spoke of each region of the country and stressed the contributions of each to the whole union. He warned the American people to be wary of influential and persuasive power brokers. He said that powerful political factions "are likely in the course of time and things, to become potent engines by which cunning, ambitious and unprincipled men will be enabled to subvert the power of the people." He did, however, make an exception to that opinion by indicating that the parties can serve as a check on the powers of the government.

Chapter 7 – The Bitterly Fought Elections

The Contested Election of 1796

In the year 1796, John Adams, the vice president under George Washington, and Thomas Pinckney—both Federalists—ran against Thomas Jefferson and Aaron Burr, the two Democratic-Republicans. As soon as the campaign was under way, an essay appeared in the *Gazette of the United States*, a Federalist newspaper. It was signed by "Phocion." It warned its readers that Thomas Jefferson was having an affair with his slave, Sally Hemings, and added that Jefferson planned on freeing all the slaves. That latter notion alone struck fear in the hearts of the Southerners, who had developed an economic dependency on slavery to support their plantations. Of course, the idea that a white man would have intercourse with an African American slave offended the sensibilities of the prejudiced. The essay also went on to accuse Jefferson of having run away from the British soldiers during battle while the courageous Alexander Hamilton stayed his ground and fought with the Patriots. Alexander Hamilton was, in fact, the person who wrote under the pseudonym "Phocion."

During the campaign, Hamilton wrote to the federal electors privately, advising them to vote for Thomas Pinckney, hoping that it would convince them to elect Pinckney rather than John Adams. Because Pinckney was from the South, he assumed that some of the Southerners would be more likely to vote for Pinckney than Adams. Hamilton's scheme was revealed to some electors before the voting took place, however. So, instead of the Northern Federalists following along with Hamilton's recommendation, they voted for Adams but withheld their second ballots from Pinckney, as each elector was given two votes. Instead, they simply left their second vote blank. There were other electors who didn't know about the scheme ahead of time, so it was estimated that Adams might have lost five votes in New Jersey and two in Connecticut.

As a result of the election, John Adams obtained 71 electoral votes, and Thomas Jefferson received 68. That wasn't the result that Hamilton expected. In addition, for the first time in U.S. history, the president and the vice president were from two different parties (back then, whoever had the highest number of votes became president while the person with the second-highest number became vice president).

The Quasi-War

John Adams was president from 1797 to 1801. During his administration, there was an undeclared war between France and America called the "Quasi-War." The Quasi-War was fought from 1798 to 1800, and it was a naval battle stemming from the forceful impressment of American sailors and the destruction of their ships. Fears of yet another war permeated the population. The administration was also obsessed with concerns that French operatives would infiltrate the country, causing Adams and the Federalist-controlled Congress to pass the Alien and Sedition Acts. Adams, in particular, knew that another war could ruin the country, and he didn't want to leave that to be his legacy. Fear of infiltration by France within the country led to a great deal of mistrust and paranoia on the part of the administration, leading them to curtail the free press. Hamilton was of the opinion that some of the editorials in the press were written by anti-American aliens. As a result of the enforcement of the Alien and Sedition Acts, innocent people who were just journalists and commentators were imprisoned as a result. The increased anxiety prevailing in the country also resurrected fears about Great Britain gaining renewed strength, which had first occurred during the vice presidency of John Adams under the Washington administration when the very unpopular Jay Treaty of 1794 was in effect. Even at this late date, there was still British influence in the unsettled lands of the Pacific Northwest.

Alexander Hamilton: Major-General

Adams also called upon George Washington, who was now retired, and asked him to organize preparations with some major officers in case there was ground combat. Although he was quite feeble at the time, Washington always answered the call of his country. Toward this effort, he traveled to Philadelphia. Washington stipulated that he choose the individual with whom he would work. Major Alexander Hamilton was then promoted to Major-General and was chosen to head up the operation. Recalling the difficulty he had getting supplies and equipment during the Revolution, Washington stressed to Hamilton that he needed to focus on that crucial aspect. Washington further gave him complete authorization to conduct operations if a ground war broke out, indicating that he himself wouldn't be physically up to the task. He then tasked Hamilton with the recruitment efforts and arrangements for the procurement of supplies.

In order to provide funding if such a war broke out, Hamilton contacted Oliver Wolcott Jr., the current secretary of the treasury, Senator Theodore Sedgwick from Massachusetts, and William Loughton Smith of the House Ways and Means Committee. The House Ways and Means Committee is a tax-writing group selected from members of the House of Representatives who decide how to go about collecting taxes. Unfortunately, Smith was asked to leave as Hamilton felt he was too slow to act and instead took on the responsibility himself. Instead of being taxed on their land, people were taxed on the number of windows they had in their houses. While this may seem strange today, glass was a valuable commodity in the early 19th century. Those who had more windows were generally wealthier. There was also another tax passed that was similar to the old Stamp Act. German farmers in southeastern Pennsylvania demonstrated against these taxes. Once the threat of war had passed, those taxes were rescinded.

The Explosive Election of 1800

This election was one of the most contentious and fiery elections in American history. Thomas Jefferson and Aaron Burr ran on the side of the Democratic-Republicans against John Adams and Charles Cotesworth Pinckney, both Federalists. Burr influenced Tammany Hall to collect donations from its membership for the campaign of Jefferson and himself and persuade electoral delegates to vote for their ticket. He also played into the Federalists' hands by becoming lukewarm about France in case some of the assemblymen were of that mind. He then saw to it that his supporters were merchants, mechanics, and workmen who would typically be attracted to Federalist candidates. Burr felt that befriending the influential people and building loyalties, especially among the assemblymen of New York, could sway an election. Jefferson's campaign workers also made many attempts to get him elected. They spoke to their influential friends and family about Jefferson's positive characteristics. Jefferson tended to do his campaigning "behind the scenes" by writing letters to those he knew. Burr, on the other hand, campaigned actively for himself. He visited Connecticut and Rhode Island, giving speeches. He said that what the country needed now was someone who could forge regional alliances between the Northern manufacturing states and the South, a person who could get Democratic-Republican support even in the Northern states. Of course, Burr was from New York, so he filled that qualification.

Since each elector had two votes, Burr stressed to the Democratic-Republicans that they should be sure to cast one vote for himself and one for Jefferson. Occasionally, electors would just vote for one man and withhold their second vote. That, he indicated, might result in Jefferson becoming president and John Adams vice president.

For the Democratic-Republicans, the key to getting the New York vote was Aaron Burr. Jefferson, however, was uncomfortable with Burr's style of campaigning. He and many others saw Burr as being selfishly ambitious. He never came across at election time as a "team player." Burr was a shrewd and calculating politician, and Jefferson felt that he really didn't hold on very tightly to Democratic-Republican values. Burr was a New Yorker who never turned a hoe in his life, so Jefferson found it hard to believe that Burr believed in the rights of the Southern farmers.

As for Hamilton, a Federalist, he had disparaged John Adams and Charles Pinckney in prior publications, but, of course, he didn't want Jefferson or Burr to win. In his published letters, Hamilton attempted to soften his formerly negative aspersions against John Adams and recommended that the Federalists vote for John Adams or Pinckney—whichever they preferred. Jefferson and Burr, meanwhile, crisscrossed New York trying to round up support.

In an effort to weaken Hamilton's role within the Federalist Party, Burr was able to secure copies of confidential letters sent to members of Congress and published sections of them in the Democratic-Republican newspapers. However, it did more than diminish support for the Federalists. It helped fracture the party. The noted statesman Rufus King said, "I have little or no doubt the letters [written by Hamilton and published by Burr] will lay the foundation of a serious opposition to General Hamilton amongst the Federalists, and that his usefulness hereafter will be greatly lessened."

It was. As a result of the 1800 election, Jefferson won 73 electoral votes, and Aaron Burr won 73. Adams won 65, and Pinckney won 64.

In the case of a tie, the responsibility passes onto the House of Representatives. In 1800, that meant the responsibility passed along to John Marshall, who was the secretary of state and who had to monitor a new election between Jefferson and Burr.

A minimum of at least nine votes from the sixteen states was needed to break the tie. Burr received votes from six of the eight states controlled by the Federalists. Seven of the states controlled by the Democratic-Republicans voted for Jefferson. Hamilton rigorously embarked on a frenzied letter-writing campaign, reminding people that he considered Burr more "dangerous" than Thomas Jefferson. Hamilton even wrote to Secretary of State John Marshall in that regard. During his frenetic attempts to prevent Aaron Burr from becoming president after this tie vote of 1800, Hamilton called Burr a "profligate, corrupt, bankrupt, and an unprincipled man" who was looking to cheat Jefferson out of the presidency. Throughout the campaign and even prior to that, Burr had heard accusations that he was an adulterer, that he forced women into prostitution, that he accepted bribes, and that he stole from the escrow funds of his legal clients. Other anonymous brief notices showed up in print that further disparaged Burr. Hamilton also wrote letters to some of the most influential Federalists he knew, including, Oliver Wolcott, Theodore Sedgwick, Gouverneur Morris, Harrison Gray Otis, John Rutledge, John Marshall, and James Bayard. As revealed in his letter to Samuel Bayard, Hamilton wrote a number of grievous negatives about Burr, going so far as to imply that Burr could become an "unruly tyrant" who would limit the liberty and freedom of the people. Bayard convinced nine Federalists not to vote for Burr, and they instead passed in blank ballots. Tie votes kept reoccurring, and the House had to hold the voting again on a number of occasions. Finally, Hamilton was able to influence the electoral voters, and as a result, Thomas Jefferson became president with Aaron Burr as the vice president.

Aftermath

The election of 1800 stimulated a lot of animosity among Americans. Adams also wrote to Abigail that his journey home would be burdened. Upon his arrival, it is said that he rushed into his farming work to distract himself. The *Philadelphia Aurora* insulted him in their columns, saying that Adams "needed to be cast like polluted water out the back door, and who should immediately leave for Quincy that Mrs. Adams may wash her befuddled brains clear."

During that same year, John Adams' son, Charles, died of alcoholism. Jefferson had received that notice accidentally and forwarded the missive to Adams, kindly expressing his sincerest condolences. It was a gentle letter full of empathy and understanding.

Now thrown into forced retirement, Adams was not only depressed, but he was also angry, and he kept ruminating about the turmoil and tribulations of this election. Abigail Adams said, "Party hatred, by its deadly poison, blinds the eyes and puts venom into the heart." As a consequence of the nastiness and insults that Jefferson engaged in during electioneering, Adams broke off his relationship with him. It wasn't until thirteen years later that they reconciled.

The Fatal Duel of Hamilton's Son, Philip

One night, in 1801, Alexander Hamilton's eldest son, nineteen-year-old Philip Hamilton, and his friend, Stephen Price, came across George Eacker and a friend attending a comedy in New York entitled *The West Indian*. Eacker was an accomplished lawyer in the city who was rising the social ladder in New York society. He had been chosen to give a speech for the Fourth of July Independence Day celebration four months earlier, which was sponsored by the Tammany Society. According to most listeners, Eacker's speech was "good," but some of the members of the Democratic-Republican society felt that there were insinuations made in the oration against the Federalist agenda. Philip and Richard were angry about the remarks made during it, and they intruded into Eacker's box seat and began taunting him about some of the supposedly offensive remarks. Then Eacker turned to Price and Philip Hamilton and quipped angrily, "It is too abominable to be publicly insulted by a set of rascals!" The term "rascal" in those days was a hot-button term that implied a challenge to a duel. To that retort, Price and Philip became even more enraged. Philip then shouted, "Who do you call damn'd rascals?"

The generally accepted procedure for a duel is to appoint "seconds," who are trusted friends to act as witnesses. It is their function to try to elicit an apology by the one who has apparently offended the honor of the other. Although movies have portrayed it, duels are never preceded by a blow or slap on the face. If the apology fails to be procured, duelists may announce in advance that they will use dummy bullets or shoot in the air, but no one says they will aim toward a less lethal area of the body. The seconds load the pistols but don't cock them, and then the pistols are presented to the duelists. Each duelist stands ten yards apart. If neither falls on the first shot, the shooting continues for two or three shots until someone falls. There are only three possible outcomes when a duel takes place: 1) One party is injured and bloodied. If that is sufficient retribution for the winner, the duel is ended. If the party isn't satisfied, the duel continues. 2) If a duelist isn't able to proceed because of a serious wound, the duel is considered over. 3) If either party is fatally killed, the duel is over.

John Church of the Schuyler family attempted to negotiate peace among the three but was unsuccessful. Two duels were scheduled— one between Stephen Prince and George Eacker and the other between Eacker (if he survived) and Philip Hamilton. Price and Eacker faced each other on November 22nd, 1801. Both shot, but both parties missed each other. The parties agreed that they were satisfied. Whenever that happened, it was the traditional practice to abandon the attempt. Alexander Hamilton, according to the *New York Evening Post*, wasn't aware of the planned duel at the time. However, historians have said that he probably did know about it, indicating that the lack of publicity was most likely an effort to protect Alexander from rumors that he was involved. Dueling, although frowned upon, isn't technically illegal in all of the states today, but if a duel did take place, people could still be convicted on charges like manslaughter. However, back then, many of the prominent politicians were against it, such as Ben Franklin, John Adams, and Thomas Jefferson. Some men who had military experience tended to practice it to settle issues and felt it was a respectable way to defend their honor and integrity.

The second duel—between Hamilton and Eacker—was scheduled for the next day later, November 23rd, 1801. It was to take place again in Weehawken, New Jersey, on a sandbar near the current Jersey City. In fact, this would be the same place where his father would later be mortally wounded in his own duel. Philip took his father's advice and didn't fire first. However, neither did Eacker. They stared at one another for a few moments before lifting their pistols. Eacker fired first, according to witnesses, hitting Philip above his right hip. The bullet went through his body, though, and actually lodged itself in his left arm. Philip fired in response, but it is possible that it was an involuntary spasm as the bullet did nothing to Eacker. Falling to the ground, Philip's face turned white as his wounds started bleeding profusely.

The young man was lowered into a rowboat and taken across the Hudson River to the home of Hamilton's sister-in-law, Angelica Church. Alexander contacted the family physician, David Hosack, and both of them raced to the scene. Philip lay on the bed all night in total delirium with his eyes darting back and forth. According to Henry Dawson, a witness to the event, Alexander fainted from grief when he arrived. Eliza, who was also there, was three months pregnant with Alexander's youngest son at the time. Friends arrived shortly. Finally, after fourteen hours spent in agony, Philip confessed his faith in Christ and died. Alexander, it was said, was so distraught that he could barely stand during the funeral service and needed his friends to hold him up. Eliza herself was inconsolable. Alexander's youngest son was named "Philip" or "Young Philip" after his deceased brother.

Alexander sunk into a deep depression for many months following the death of his son. His close friends said it took him months to reply to the many sympathy letters he received after the event. He had been very close to Philip and raised him to follow his own beliefs. Philip, it was said, was very much like his father, so it's no surprise that he reacted so vehemently to Eacker's comments.

After Philip's death, his sister, Angelica who was only seventeen years old, had a mental breakdown. The psychiatrist, also a relative, said, "Upon receipt of the news of her brother's death in the Eacker duel, she suffered so great a shock that her mind became permanently impaired, and although taken care of by her devoted mother for a long time, there was no amelioration in her condition."

Chapter 8 – Bottom of the Curve

While Alexander Hamilton wasn't a strong supporter of Jefferson, he did recognize that Jefferson had integrity and was devoted to his principles. After the Federalist Party started to weaken, Senator Gouverneur Morris of New York was cognizant of Hamilton's position after the 1800 election. He wrote in 1801 and said that Hamilton appeared to be in "the awkward situation of a man who continues sober after the company are drunk." About Burr, Morris said, "Thus you see that Mr. Burr is resolved to preserve himself in a situation to adhere to his former friends, engagements, and projects; and to use the Federalists as the tool of his aggrandizement."

Hostility continued to brew between the Federalists and the Democratic-Republicans. Each party had their respective reasons for doing so, but the political crisis only continued to grow. Everyone was looking for a scapegoat. The Democratic-Republicans, in particular, were worried about what the Federalists might do. Rumors of violence permeated the taverns and parlors.

George Washington didn't declare a political party affiliation, although many of his viewpoints and decisions were similar to the Federalist agenda. In fact, many people referred to him as a

Federalist. His successor, Adams, was a declared Federalist. After the election, all eyes looked toward Jefferson as a Democratic-Republican to ascertain the differences in how the parties ran the country. The Democratic-Republicans were more interested in a protectionist position, which would generally remove America from the world stage and focus upon agrarianism and development within the country itself. Predictably, Thomas Jefferson decreased government expenditures, thus lowering excise taxes, giving relief to the companies and farmers involved in the manufacture and distribution of whiskey and the sale of other goods among the states. Progress had finally been made toward the repayment of war debts, due to the efforts of Hamilton. In addition, the reduction in government spending would leave even more money available for private enterprise. During the initial phase of his presidency, Jefferson reduced the size of the United States Navy as well as other related expenses. That alone reduced the national debt from 83 to 57 million dollars. Now American shipping could be of a commercial rather than a military nature.

Under Jefferson, Albert Gallatin was appointed the secretary of the treasury. With Jefferson's approval, Gallatin followed through with much of the same policies established by Alexander Hamilton, who had preceded him.

The War of the Barbary Pirates

That relief was incredibly short-lived, though. Jefferson, as foreign minister under Washington, had negotiated with the Barbary pirates, the largest piracy operation in the southern Mediterranean. A treaty was made with the Barbary state of Morocco in 1784. Although it did involve paying tributes to the pirates, it seemed to preserve the peace with the exception of Algiers and the Tripoli pirates. In 1801, just after Jefferson took office, the Dey of Algiers demanded a tribute of one million dollars every year. Also, in 1801, the Pasha of Tripoli demanded 225,000 dollars, but Jefferson refused to spend more. For the protection of American shipping, Jefferson asked Congress to allocate money to send over one schooner and then six frigates to protect the merchant vessels. His new secretary of state, James Madison, wrote to the Pasha of Tripoli, indicating to him that it was the president's intention to send this initial squadron over to negotiate peace, but that failed when the Pasha of Tripoli declared war on the United States. Jefferson approached Congress with a request for the funds to finance this mission and obtained it under the "Act for the protection of commerce and seamen of the United States against the Tripolitan Cruisers." Hamilton disagreed with Jefferson's solution, arguing that a formal declaration of war needed to be passed by Congress. Jefferson ignored that and asked his newly appointed secretary of war, Henry Dearborn, to intercede. Dearborn argued with the president, but there was no time for prolonged debate, so Jefferson himself sent Commander Edward Preble to go to Sicily to obtain the support of King Ferdinand of Spain and secure the use of gunboats and two warships. Because of this, Jefferson had been forced to break his promise to reduce the size of the navy.

Jefferson's newly appointed secretary of the navy, Robert Smith, sent more ships under Commander Preble, including the *Chesapeake*, *Argus*, *Constellation*, *Constitution*, *Enterprise*, and *Philadelphia*. The American ships set up a blockade of the Barbary ports and raided the pirates' ships. In 1803, during the naval maneuvers in the Mediterranean, Captain Bainbridge, his ship the *Philadelphia*, and his men were kidnapped and taken prisoner. In retaliation, Lieutenant Decatur stole aboard a Tripoli ship and captured it. Ground forces were disembarked and marched across North Africa all the way to the Tripolitan city of Derna, where the Barbary soldiers were defeated.

The Great Louisiana Purchase of 1803

The Seven Years' War between England and France and its allies, which lasted between 1756 and 1763, was mostly a European conflict which spilled over into the British Colonies before the American Revolution. One of the phases of it was known as the French and Indian War, which was waged between the British Americans and the French, both with their Native American allies.

The goal was to control this vast amount of land amounting to about 828,000 square miles west of the Mississippi River. After the Seven Years' War was over, the secretive treaty, the Treaty of Fontainebleau in 1762, ceded the territory to Spain. After American independence, the United States obtained the rights to use the Mississippi River for navigation and shipment of goods to and from the Port of New Orleans, which was still owned by Spain. Until 1798, the Americans were permitted to store goods there until they were shipped overseas or somewhere more local.

In 1800, Spain, in need of funds, was in the process of transferring the Louisiana territory and New Orleans back to France. Jefferson had long coveted this land as he could expand the United States westward and create more states there. So, he sent Robert Livingston, his U.S. minister to France, to open up negotiations in 1801. The Port of New Orleans, in particular, was essential for American trade.

Napoleon Bonaparte now had control of France, and he sent in a military force to protect it. The Southerners were also afraid that Napoleon would free all of the slaves in Louisiana, which might cause slave revolts in the Southern states. The opposite happened. Napoleon wanted the wealth in the islands of the Caribbean more. In 1802, General Charles Leclerc was sent to Saint-Dominique and reestablished slavery. British and Spanish forces became involved in a conflict over Saint- Dominique and its nearby islands. Concerned that hostilities would break out between the French and the settlers already there, Jefferson declared neutrality. The people on Saint-Dominique managed to secure a victory, declaring independence under the new name of Haiti in 1804.

Jefferson quietly worked with a French noble by the name of Pierre Samuel du Pont de Nemours. Du Pont was living in the United States at the time, but he was able to contact Napoleon directly, and Jefferson wanted to know what Napoleon's intentions were in regards to the Territory of Louisiana. Without informing Livingston, his foreign minister to France, Jefferson sent James Monroe over there in 1803. Napoleon attempted to regain control of the all-important island of Saint-Dominque but was met with extreme resistance. Already, Napoleon had lost a little over 24,000 to 25,000 men out of the original 31,000 sent there during the aforementioned expedition to Saint-Dominque alone, and he was growing weary of trying to conduct a war on two fronts—one on the European continent and another one across the Atlantic Ocean. Also, because Napoleon couldn't control Saint-Dominque, no sugar shipments would be forthcoming, which was their prime commodity there. Since he wouldn't have sufficient revenues from the colonies, he didn't see much of a point of holding onto Louisiana. Plus, Spain had yet to finish the transfer of the territory to him, so Napoleon might have been spurred on by spite, selling something to the United States that wasn't even his quite yet.

In 1803, just a few days before James Monroe's arrival, the treasury minister of France, François Barbé-Marbois approached Robert Livingston and offered to sell not just New Orleans but all of the Louisiana Territory to Jefferson. Jefferson was astonished that Napoleon was willing to sell that much land and raised his initial offer from ten million dollars for New Orleans to fifteen million dollars for the Louisiana territory. That would be equivalent to about 600 billion dollars today, and acquiring the territory doubled the size of the United States.

Hamilton approved of this purchase wholeheartedly and even complimented Jefferson for agreeing to this sale. Several months before the treaty was ratified, Hamilton wrote, "This, it will be allowed, is an important acquisition not indeed as a territory, but as being essential to the peace of prosperity of our western country, and as opening a free and valuable market to our commercial states." The treaty was ratified on May 2nd, 1803.

Political Partisanship: Trial of Samuel Chase

Aaron Burr, Jefferson's vice president, was bypassed in terms of having an intimate role in the Jefferson Cabinet, besides presiding over the 1803 impeachment trial of Justice Samuel Chase, whom Jefferson perceived as his political enemy. Chase heavily supported the Federalists but made the error of carrying on a political soliloquy from the bench against the Democratic-Republicans. He said to the grand jury that the country was "headed down the road to mobocracy, the worst of all governments," and he implicated that the Democratic-Republicans would extinguish all liberty and freedom. Jefferson wrote to Representative Joseph Nicholson, indicating that Chase should be charged with seditious behavior. The three charges had to do with comments stemming from Chase's conduct during the treason trial of John Fries during the Whiskey Rebellion and the trial of James Callender on libel charges, as well as the vicious comments he made about the Democratic-Republicans, mentioned above, to a grand jury in Baltimore. In his earlier Federalist letters under the name of "Publius," Hamilton had been very critical of Samuel Chase, even though he was a Federalist. Hamilton felt that he was corrupt and used his position to aggrandize his own reputation.

Although political partisanship was rampant during the campaign for the 1800 election for president, it was not intended to be practiced by a Supreme Court Justice. However, in 1804, this was not as strictly practiced as it is today. Samuel Chase was opposed to the repeal of the Judiciary Act of 1801, an act which restricted the members of the Supreme Court in such a way that they could be chosen according to the party that was in office. Chase, it was alleged, showed seditious behavior when he lambasted the Democratic-Republicans from the bench. If he was convicted, that would mean that he had committed a "high crime and misdemeanor." In order for that to happen, two-thirds of the jury had to choose to convict him.

As a Democratic-Republican, Burr wasn't sympathetic with Chase, but he strictly observed court etiquette in the execution of his role of presiding over the trial. Although Chase was old and frail, Senator William Plumer of New Hampshire observed that Burr insisted that Chase find his own seat, as was customary, and not be provided with the table he had requested. Plumer said, "Although rightfully concerned about maintaining an atmosphere of judicial decorum, Burr had lost much of his 'easy grace' and consummate tact that made him an effective presiding officer." Curiously, attendees in the courtroom were also snacking on cake and apples, but Burr said he didn't notice that when it was brought up.

As was his practice, Burr was impartial when passing judgment. He indicated that the criteria for impeachment wasn't met, and Samuel Chase was freed.

The Election of 1804

Jefferson began to suspect that Burr was only aligned with the Democratic-Republicans because he felt that he would gain political ground by doing so. Jefferson was also astonished that Burr didn't graciously step down in favor of Jefferson during the 1800 election.

Due to the results of the 1800 elections, the Twelfth Amendment to the U.S. Constitution was passed in June 1804, just in time for the new presidential election. Under this amendment, one would cast a vote for the president and another vote for the vice president—in other words, the person who won the second most votes would no longer be automictically vice president. Jefferson, of course, was going to run again as president, but he did not choose Burr to be his running mate; instead, he chose George Clinton

Running for the Federalists was Charles Cotesworth Pinckney, a Southerner who ran previously in the 1800 election. He was chosen because he was a planter who contributed during the administration of John Adams and the Quasi-War. Rufus King, a well-respected lawyer who served Jefferson despite the fact that he was a Federalist, ran as his running mate.

Due to the strong economic status of the county, the Louisiana Purchase, and Jefferson's own popularity, he easily won the presidency, attaining 162 electoral votes to Pinckney's 14 votes.

The 1804 New York Gubernatorial Race

Jefferson's suspicions about Burr were correct. Instead of being a loyal Democratic-Republican, Burr also campaigned among the Federalists against Morgan Lewis in the 1804 New York gubernatorial election. Lewis came from a respectable military background, as did Burr, and was an assemblyman in New York in 1789 and 1792. George Clinton was New York's previous governor and was very popular. However, now that he would be Jefferson's running mate in the presidential election, he was no longer a political threat. The seat was wide open.

Even though Burr was a Democratic-Republican, he had supporters among the Federalists, especially a splinter group called the Essex Junto, which was made up of powerful politicians from the New England states. Several years prior to this, they had offered Hamilton a position in a clandestine plot to separate New England from the union. Hamilton refused to participate, but word had it that Burr indicated he might be interested in this. Hamilton told the Federalists that the result of voting for Burr might be a "dismemberment of the Union." According to Hamilton, Burr could then become chief of the "Northern portion" and might be a "despotic chief." Hamilton also said Burr was a man of "irregular and insatiable ambition." Hamilton then added that his political rival, John Lansing, would be a better governor because he could keep New York united.

In February of 1804, Hamilton gave a speech to that effect to his fellow Federalists in Albany. Hamilton always was a charismatic and respected individual. Just a few months before the gubernatorial election was held, Lansing decided not to run and was replaced by Morgan Lewis. Burr ran as an independent, but he had the support of many at Tammany Hall as well as the radical Federalists. Lewis, on the other hand, wasn't associated with Tammany Hall, but he had the backing of the former Democratic-Republican governor, Clinton.

A little over 58 percent of the "Clintonian" Democratic-Republicans voted for Lewis, and he won the election. Burr received almost 42 percent of the vote.

The Duel Between Alexander Hamilton and Aaron Burr

In early 1804, at a dinner party at Judge John Tayler's home, both Tayler and Hamilton dreaded the possibility that Aaron Burr might be elected governor of New York. James Kent, another illustrious Federalist who was at the table, expressed the same fear. Dr. Charles Cooper, another guest, then characterized Burr as a "dangerous man and one who ought not to be trusted with the reins of government." Cooper wrote that in a letter which ended up being printed in the *New York Evening Post* in July of that year. It wasn't uncommon for letters to be intercepted and deliberately misdirected to the press.

When that letter hit the light, Cooper was peppered with questions. On one occasion, Cooper was quoted to have said, "I could detail to you a still more despicable opinion which General Hamilton has expressed of Mr. Burr." Cooper's letter was reprinted in the *Albany Register* on April 24th, 1804, and when Burr read it, he lost his temper and shot off a letter to Alexander Hamilton.

Hamilton responded that the language of Dr. Cooper "plainly implies that he considered this opinion of you, which he attributes to me, as a 'despicable' one; but he affirms that I have expressed some other still 'more despicable' without however mentioning to whom, when or where." Then Hamilton said that between gentlemen, the distinction between the words "despicable" and "more despicable" weren't worthy of discussion.

Hamilton didn't respond to Burr's reply right away, so Burr wrote more letters. Other letters then went back and forth between the two. Burr's communications were full of free-floating anger and evidence of the increasing paranoia of a man who was now obsessing over a word.

In these letters, the term "honor" was often mentioned. That was a cue used to signify a duel. Even though the practice had been forbidden by state laws in both New Jersey and New York, it wasn't well enforced in the former state. One of the most common places for duels was Weehawken, New Jersey, in the heights near the Palisades, the same place where Philip Hamilton had his duel three years before. This wasn't a heavily trafficked area, and a duel was scheduled there for July 11th, 1804. Both groups rowed across the Hudson River separately, and Burr's group arrived first. William Peter Van Ness, a federal judge, stood for Aaron Burr and Nathaniel Pendleton, a New York judge, stood for Alexander Hamilton. Hamilton's group arrived about a half hour later, whose boat also included a physician, Dr. David Hosack.

It was common for the two combatants to deliberately miss their first shot, shooting at the ground to demonstrate their courage in participating in a duel at all. After this shot, the duel could then come to an end. Although they could fire again, few did, and usually, both left and called the matter closed. Because the people who stood in as seconds had their backs turned, they couldn't see exactly what happened. In the early morning hours of July 11th, 1804, two shots cracked out, breaking the deadly silence. Van Ness and Pendleton swung around and saw Hamilton lying in a heap upon the dusty ground, bleeding profusely from his abdomen.

Hosack later related that Hamilton regained consciousness only briefly after he applied smelling salts. He told Doctor Hosack, "I did not intend to fire at him." Then he told the doctor he had lost all feeling in his lower limbs and said no more. He was carried by boat to the Greenwich Village home of William Bayard Jr., a New York banker, and died there the following morning after receiving communion from Bishop Benjamin Moore. All his seven living children and his loving wife Eliza were there at his bedside when he breathed his last.

There are a few versions told about the duel, and it was said that Hamilton aimed above Burr's head, prompting Burr to think that

Hamilton was shooting at him; others said that he fired into the ground, which was the more traditional way. The newspapers reported that a ball was later found to have gone through the limb of a cedar tree about thirteen feet above Burr's head, but some claim that Hamilton's pistol went off accidentally when he fell.

The country went into a frenzy over the duel. There was disagreement over who shot who first and whether or not the duel would have been resolved with an apology by Hamilton. For the most part, people considered Burr to be a murderer. Hamilton was popular, and many hung on to his every word when he published his opinions about American issues. The newspapers which leaned toward the Democratic-Republican faction, however, had difficulty defending Burr, so instead, they targeted the Federalist press for its campaign assailing the reputation of Burr. During those years, this duel indicated that party politics was not only vicious but also violent.

There is one rock at the duel site called the "Death Rock," upon which it is said Hamilton's head was propped up after the duel. Alexander Hamilton is buried at the Trinity Churchyard in lower Manhattan.

The Destiny of Aaron Burr

Both Hamilton and Burr were at the bottom of the curve in their political careers at the time of Hamilton's death, but Burr had new and exciting plans for the future. Aaron Burr hadn't forgotten the appeal from the radical Federalists in 1800 who proposed a secession of the New England states from the union. It wasn't the first time this kind of notion crossed his mind. In 1795 and again in 1796, he had proposed that America invade some of the Spanish lands in Texas. He knew the Spanish didn't have the disciplined military that the British had. After seeing that Jefferson was able to gain acres of land from France at the Louisiana Purchase, he visited some areas there in 1805. While exploring the region, he met Harman Biennerhasset, a lawyer, who owned a lot of land in the Ohio River valley. He also met with a former Continental Army officer, James Wilkinson, and hired him along with Biennerhasset to help conquer the Spanish-owned territory of south Texas and part of Mexico. Burr wanted to cede from the union and set up his own private empire in that fertile area. Burr didn't have access to a lot of funding, so he contacted an Englishman by the name of Anthony Merry, with whom he discussed ideas about attracting the interest of the British in American territory west of the Mississippi. Although he tried, Merry wasn't very influential in Britain and couldn't attract their interest. Following that, Burr and his companions went about recruiting men for a force.

Burr's conspiracy came to the attention of President Thomas Jefferson, and in 1807, Burr was put on trial for treason. The prosecution asserted that Burr's plan for land acquisition included some land that was a part of the Louisiana Purchase of 1803. However, it was discovered during the trial that the document upon which they based the evidence was an uncorroborated letter from one of Burr's alleged conspirators, John Wilkinson, so the court threw out this solitary piece of evidence, and Burr was acquitted.

After the case, Burr fled for Europe, living there from 1808 to 1812. Upon his return to New York, he reopened his law practice in order to pay some of his past debts, which were substantial. He lived in relative obscurity, using the pseudonym "Edwards," his mother's maiden name, when he could. He married again in 1833, but the marriage only lasted a few short months. In 1834, Burr died of a massive stroke.

The Hamilton Progeny Lived On

Although Hamilton's daughter, Angelica, had suffered a mental breakdown after the death of Hamilton's eldest son, her younger brother, Alexander Jr., attended Columbia College and then began the study of law as his father had done. He was also a military man like his father and later resumed the practice of law, becoming a federal attorney, a legislator, and later on a realtor. Likewise,

Hamilton's fourth child, James, had a similar career in the military and law. He married Mary Morris, the daughter of Robert Morris, a financier of the Revolution whom his parents knew well. Curiously, James differed with his father's views on banking and opposed national banks to service the government and was a heavy supporter of Thomas Jefferson. It's interesting to note that he named his main residence the "Nevis House" after his father's birthplace.

On the morning before Alexander Hamilton's fateful duel, he called for his twelve-year-old son, John Church Hamilton. Related in his later years, John Hamilton said that on that day, he drew John close and "taking my hands in his palms, all four hands extended, he told me to repeat the Lord's Prayer." In 1834, John Church Hamilton wrote a biography of his father's life.

Alexander's son, William, was only six years old at the time of the duel. When he became an adult, he moved to Illinois and was involved in the legislature for a while. Later on, he became a lead miner of all things. Little Eliza, who was four when her father died, cared for her mother until her death in 1854. "Young Phil," who was the youngest, was said to have "manifested much of his father's sweetness and happy disposition, and was always notably considerate of the feelings of others, and was punctilious to a fault in is obligations."

Conclusion

In August 2015, the musical *Hamilton* opened on Broadway. One of the most notable quotes from that performance was "How does a bastard, orphan, son of a whore and a Scotsman, dropped in the middle of a forgotten spot in the Caribbean by providence, impoverished, in squalor grow up to be a hero and a scholar?" One might simply respond that America was a land of liberty that supported the rights of the individual, regardless of their social standing. That is true, to an extent, but it takes more than rugged individualism to become universally recognized as a Founding Father of the United States. It takes extraordinary courage to rise above one's social station in life and reach for what seems to surpass one's own abilities.

Hamilton was a soldier with unmitigated valor during the American Revolution because he felt his beliefs and those of his countrymen were worth dying for. Hamilton's credo was like the U.S. Constitution itself, which was wrapped up in his astute mind—the mind of a man convinced in the ideals of the new American nation. He was, however, a stubborn man who argued with his learned contemporaries like John Adams, the second president of the country, and the third president, Thomas Jefferson. Unlike many of the other Founding Fathers, Hamilton was never wealthy, but that never stopped him from expressing his views when he wrote essays for *The Federalist Papers*. For a man who wasn't wealthy, he understood finances and managed to pull America out of debt after the war and resolve a banking crisis.

As he looked upon the possibility of death, Hamilton knew he would never be president because of his affair with Maria Reynolds. So, he planned to go where destiny would lead—to a life of being a campaigner extraordinaire and what is today called a "power broker." Just that, and nothing more. Hamilton's words spoken hundreds of years ago to thousands of patriotic Americans will never fade from the language of liberty, freedom, and, above all, truth. Hamilton once said, "I thought it my duty to exhibit things as they are, not as they ought to be." And that is the way it was on that fateful day of July 11th, 1804.

Read more biographies from Captivating History

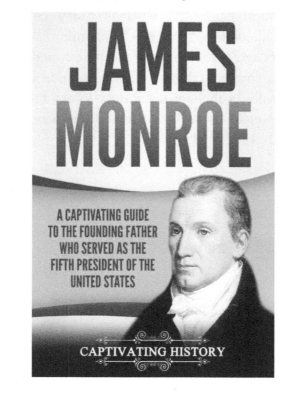

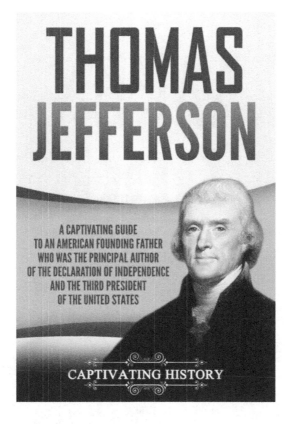

THOMAS
JEFFERSON

A CAPTIVATING GUIDE
TO AN AMERICAN FOUNDING FATHER
WHO WAS THE PRINCIPAL AUTHOR
OF THE DECLARATION OF INDEPENDENCE
AND THE THIRD PRESIDENT
OF THE UNITED STATES

CAPTIVATING HISTORY

Bibliography

Newton, Michael (2015) *Alexander Hamilton: The Formative Years.* Eletheria Publishing

Chernow, R. (2004) *Hamilton.* Penguin Books

Palmotto, M. (2014) *Combatting Human Trafficking: A Multidisciplinary Approach.* CRC Press

Clark, A., M.D. (2005) *Cipher/Code of Dishonor; Aaron Burr: An American Enigma.* AuthorHouse

Jenkinson, I. (2019) *Aaron Burr, His Personal and Political Relations with Thomas Jefferson and Alexander Hamilton.* Wentworth Press

Hamilton, A. "Hamilton, A. Letters," Retrieved from https://founders.archives.gov/documents/Hamilton/01-25-02-0169

"Burr-Hamilton Duel," Retrieved from https://www.britannica.com/event/Burr-Hamilton-duel

"Aaron Burr," Retrieved from http://www.americaslibrary.gov/jb/nation/jb_nation_hamburr_1.html

"Election of 1800," Retrieved from https://lehrmaninstitute.org/history/1800.html#burr

"Biography of Aaron Burr," Retrieved from https://www.britannica.com/biography/Aaron-Burr

"Biography of Alexander Hamilton," Retrieved from https://www.britannica.com/biography/Aexander-Hamilton

"Bitterly Contested Presidential Election of 1800," Retrieved from https://constitutioncenter.org/blog/on-this-day-the-first-bitter-contested-presidential-election-takes-place

"Alexander Hamilton," Retrieved from https://history.howstuffworks.com/historical-figures/alexander-hamilton3.htm

Broadus, M. (1957) *Hamilton: Youth to Maturity 1755-1788.* The Free Press

Hamilton, A. "To the Royal Danish American Gazette," manuscript Library of Congress

Hamilton, A. "Report on Manufactures," manuscript Library of Congress

Randall, W. (2010) *Hamilton: A Life.* Harper Collins

Syrett, H. & Cooke, J., eds. (1987) *The Papers of Hamilton, 27 vols.* Columbia University Press

Made in the USA
Las Vegas, NV
19 December 2022

63262974R00069